Transnational Identities on Okinawa's Military Bases

"Although about a relatively small population, Zulueta's thoughtful and eye opening study of Filipino-Okinawan 'Nisei,' in addition to introducing us to this largely unstudied group of migrants, sheds light on a huge range of larger issues having to do with the nature and dynamics of identity, nationality, citizenship, international and intercultural mobility, the status of Okinawa, Japan's relationship with the US and its military, and the country's changing relations with the Philippines in post-World War II and contemporary Japan, all while maintaining an ongoing dialogue with the extant general literature on migration and migrant identity. A fascinating read."
—Lonny Carlile, *Director, Center for Japanese Studies, University of Hawaii at Manoa, USA*

"Johanna Zulueta has conducted over a decade of deep research in the 'contact zone' of Okinawa. Through the stories of individuals of mixed Okinawan and Filipino descent she illuminates the issues of identity and belonging that are integral to the experience of migration."
—Vera Mackie, *Senior Professor of Asian and International Studies, University of Wollongong, Australia*

"Johanna deciphers the entanglements in work and life between the US military, Okinawan communities, and the Filipino-Okinawan minority through an insightful close-up look at local life-courses."
—Gabriele Vogt, *Professor, Ludwig Maximilian University Munich, Germany*

Johanna O. Zulueta

Transnational Identities on Okinawa's Military Bases

Invisible Armies

Johanna O. Zulueta
Soka University
Hachioji City, Tokyo, Japan

ISBN 978-981-32-9786-9   ISBN 978-981-32-9787-6 (eBook)
https://doi.org/10.1007/978-981-32-9787-6

© The Editor(s) (if applicable) and The Author(s) 2020
This work is subject to copyright. All rights are solely and exclusively licensed by the Publisher, whether the whole or part of the material is concerned, specifically the rights of translation, reprinting, reuse of illustrations, recitation, broadcasting, reproduction on microfilms or in any other physical way, and transmission or information storage and retrieval, electronic adaptation, computer software, or by similar or dissimilar methodology now known or hereafter developed.
The use of general descriptive names, registered names, trademarks, service marks, etc. in this publication does not imply, even in the absence of a specific statement, that such names are exempt from the relevant protective laws and regulations and therefore free for general use.
The publisher, the authors and the editors are safe to assume that the advice and information in this book are believed to be true and accurate at the date of publication. Neither the publisher nor the authors or the editors give a warranty, express or implied, with respect to the material contained herein or for any errors or omissions that may have been made. The publisher remains neutral with regard to jurisdictional claims in published maps and institutional affiliations.

Cover illustration: Archistoric / Alamy Stock Photo

This Palgrave Macmillan imprint is published by the registered company Springer Nature Singapore Pte Ltd.
The registered company address is: 152 Beach Road, #21-01/04 Gateway East, Singapore 189721, Singapore

In loving memory of my father, Juanito Sison Zulueta. You were always supportive and proud of my academic endeavours and was so looking forward to reading this book. Alas, you suddenly had to return to your Creator while I was finishing this book. Thank you for everything, Papa.

Acknowledgements

As a young graduate student in the early 2000s, I had been interested in issues of ethnic identity—how people define themselves and how their identities are also ascribed by society. As a person of Chinese descent, I have always grappled with my background; but as someone who has been detached from her "Chineseness"—one who is totally not familiar with her heritage and does not even speak a word of Chinese—I saw myself in a seemingly liminal space, one whose physical features point to her Chinese ancestry, but one who is ignorant of her cultural heritage. While it may have been common sense to study more about my heritage, I took to the study of Japan to try to answer questions about ethnicity and identity. More so, my interest expanded beyond issues of ethnic identity, which led me to explore Japan's peripheries and its marginal spaces, in particular, Okinawa.

My interest in Okinawa began "accidentally" in 2003, when I was introduced to the Philippine Okinawan Society (POS) by my adviser, Nagai Hiroko, of the Ateneo de Manila University. The POS is an organization founded in 1982 by Okinawan women who travelled to the Philippines as wives of Filipino men stationed in U.S. military bases in Okinawa. Incidentally, I chose to study their offspring—half-Okinawan, half-Filipino individuals and analysed their identity constructions. They call themselves Nisei, to indicate their identity as second-generation Okinawans.

I continued to explore this group of individuals when I decided to embark on my doctoral study in 2005, at Hitotsubashi University in Tokyo. Under the guidance of my supervisor, Iyotani Toshio, I was encouraged to look into migration processes between Okinawa and the Philippines during the post-war years and problematize the significance of the Occupation in this migration scheme. In my trips to Okinawa for fieldwork, I found out that a large percentage of these Nisei have gone back to Okinawa as adults to work on U.S. military bases. However, this significant migration to Okinawa has been overlooked and overshadowed, not to mention, under-researched. I continued working on Okinawa-Philippines migration well until my postdoctoral years as a Japan Society for the Promotion of Science Fellow based at Hitotsubashi's Transnational Sociology Programme, under the tutelage of Ito Ruri. After several conference presentations and publications for almost 15 years, I realized that I had to sit and write a book about these individuals who deserve to be recognized for their place in the whole post-war and contemporary story of Okinawa.

Writing a book while working full-time as a university professor is a daunting task, where I had to balance teaching, research, and administrative work, while combatting procrastination and self-doubt. Nevertheless, the countless individuals who supported me throughout the years made me recognize the importance of producing a book on this topic; not so much so as an evaluation of one's research performance, but more so to give a voice to these people who have been "invisible" in this whole transnational project of military basing in Okinawa. Thus, I spent my summers and spring breaks working on-and-off on this project. I also benefitted from the time I spent at the Hawke Research Institute (HRI) at the University of South Australia in Adelaide as a visiting fellow under the Kantoh Sociological Society-HRI Fellowship Grant I received in 2015–2016, which enabled me to stay a month at the HRI from February to March 2016, where I worked on early versions of this manuscript.

Meanwhile, I would like to thank the following people who shared their lives with me and who continue to welcome me on my numerous visits to Okinawa: Romeo and Mina Medoruma, David Itokazu, Yagi Tsunekazu, University of the Ryukyus Emeritus Professor Kinjo Hiroyuki, Sally Oshiro, Linda Añonuevo, Victor Shiroma, Cesar Manacsa, Susan Galliguez, Manuel Yamakawa, Linda Miyazato, Sergio Uezu, Takenobu "Bhoy" Kinjo, Emilio Javier, and Crispin Aquino, as well as the Nisei parishioners at Oroku Catholic Church in Naha City, who always welcome me with open arms whenever I visit. Kenneth Alfaro and Ruby Bermillo—my sansei friends—never failed to make me laugh and remind myself to take time off to relax from research and fieldwork. Thank you for your stories and for keeping me sane during my stays in Okinawa.

Pedro Iacobelli—friend and colleague, and my sempai in book publishing—gave valuable comments on some chapters of the book as well as on the book proposal I earlier submitted. Muchas gracias for all the advice and support. Swati Vohra—graduate student at Soka University—helped me with the indexing and proofreading of the manuscript. I am so grateful for your assistance.

Sara Crowley-Vigneau—senior commissioning editor at Palgrave Macmillan—gave her utmost support in this project. I am so thankful for your belief in this endeavour. Connie Li—senior editorial assistant at Springer Nature—has guided me every step of the way until the publication of this manuscript. Thank you so much.

Throughout the years, I have presented some of the chapters in this book in numerous conferences, seminars, and workshops and I would like to thank those who gave valuable comments and questions that helped shape the overall discussion in the book. In June 2018, Hasumi Jiro of Kyushu University invited me to present my work in his graduate seminar. I would like to express my gratitude to him and his students for the opportunity to present an early version of this manuscript. Nagano Yoshiko of Kanagawa University invited me to speak at the symposium, *Shokuminchi Kokka to Kindaisei* (The Colonial State and Modernity) at Kanagawa University's Hakone Centre in March 2019, and I thank her for the valuable occasion to talk about my book project to her and her colleagues.

I would like to acknowledge funding support from the *Shibusawa Minzokugaku Shinkō Kikin*, Research Grant for Graduate Students received in 2010–2011, as well as the Grants-in-Aid for Scientific Research (KAKENHI) for JSPS Fellows (Project number 11F01314) received in 2011–2013. My subsequent visits to Okinawa were made possible by funding from the Soka University Research Promotion Funds received in 2015–2016 and 2017–2018.

I also would like to thank the Okinawa prefectural government under the stewardship of Governor Tamaki Denny for allowing me to reproduce the map of the U.S. Military Facilities in Okinawa. The Labour Management Organization for USFJ Employees (LMO/IAA) also allowed me to reproduce material from their website on the USFJ employees.

Chapter 3 is based on my chapter titled, "The Occupying Other: Third Country Nationals and the U.S. Bases in Okinawa", published in the book, *Rethinking Postwar Okinawa: Beyond American Occupation*, edited by Pedro Iacobelli and Hiroko Matsuda (2017). Chapters 4, 5, and 7 are derived in part from an article published in *Social Identities* (2017) copyright Taylor & Francis, available online: https://www.tandfonline.com/doi/full/10.1080/13504630.2017.1310037.

Lastly, I would like to thank my family back home in the Philippines for their love and support.

I hold sole responsibility for all errors and/or inaccuracies that may appear in this book.

Contents

1 **Behind the Barbed Wire Fence**   1
    Migrations and the U.S. Bases in Okinawa   6
    Military Bases and Civilian Workers   8
    Return and the Nisei   10
    Capital, Networks, and Transnational Identities   12
    The Research   14
    Organization of the Book   15
    References   19

2 **Military Bases in East Asia: The Case of Okinawa**   21
    Overseas Bases of the U.S. Military   22
    The Post-War Years and the Occupation of Okinawa   25
    The U.S. Bases in Present-day Okinawa   31
    References   35

3 **Transnational Movements During the Occupation of Okinawa: Third Country Nationals and the U.S. Bases**   39
    TCNs and the Global Hierarchy of Base Work   41
    The Entry of TCNs in Occupied Okinawa   44
    Being the "Other" Occupier: Situating the TCN   49
    Stratification and Racialization of Base Work in Occupied Okinawa   50
    References   54

4	**The "Other" Mixed Race: The Nisei in Perspective**	57
	Issei, Nisei, Sansei	58
	Understanding the Nisei: Migrations and Ethnic Group Formation	59
	"Mixed" Identities in Contemporary Okinawa	62
	The "Other" to the Amerasian	63
	Re-racialization in Japan/Okinawa	66
	Space and Time in the Re-racialization of Mixed Identities	67
	References	70
5	**The Return to Okinawa: Capital, Networks, Mobility**	73
	The Concept of Return in Migration	73
	Returns as Heuristic	75
	Return Migration as a Circumstantial Option	77
	Nationality Acquisition of the Nisei	80
	Those Who Remained	84
	References	85
6	**The Other Army: United States Forces in Japan Employees in Okinawa**	87
	USFJ Employees in Okinawa	90
	Off-Base Work in Okinawa	94
	References	97
7	**"Home Is where the Heart Is?" An Invisible Minority**	99
	The Question of Home	99
	"Home" as "Place"; "Home" as "Consciousness"	100
	Narrating Home	102
	An Invisible Minority in Okinawan Society	105
	A "Minority Within a Minority"	107
	Home and Homes; Home and Roots	108
	"Home" and "Homing"	112
	References	115

8	**Future Trajectories: A Conclusion**	117
	Nisei Futures	117
	Okinawan Society and the U.S. Bases	120
	Looking Beyond the Barbed Wire Fence	122
	References	124

Index   125

Notes on Japanese Words and Names

Japanese words and names that have prolonged or extended vowel sounds are indicated by a macron (i.e. ō). Translations of Japanese words are given in parenthesis whenever these words appear for the first time in the text. Japanese words are italicized throughout the texts, except for words that are used as concept (i.e. Nisei).

Japanese names that appear in the text are written following the Japanese way of writing, with the last name preceding the given (or first) name, except for sources written in English by Japanese authors, where I write the author's first name before his/her surname. Pseudonyms are used to identify my informants to protect their privacy.

Place names (e.g. Tokyo, Ryukyu) as well as some surnames (e.g. Ota, Oshiro) are written in their common Anglicized forms.

Abbreviations

AAFES	Army and Air Force Exchange Services
AFILJAN	Association of Filipino Japanese Nationals
EDCA	Enhanced Defence Cooperation Agreement
FILCOMRI	Filipino Community of the Ryukyu Islands
GRI	Government of the Ryukyu Islands
HNS	Host Nation Support
ICRRA	Immigration Control and Refugee Recognition Act
IHA	Indirect Hire Agreement
LMO/IAA	Labour Management Organization Incorporated Administrative Agency
LN	Local National
MC	Mariner's Contract
MCCS	Marine Corps Community Services
MLC	Master Labour Contract
PHILRYCOM	Philippines-Ryukyus Command
POS	Philippine Okinawan Society
PX	Post-exchange
SOFA	Status of Forces Agreement
TCN	Third Country National
USCAR	United States Civil Administration of the Ryukyus
USFJ	United States Forces in Japan

List of Figures

Fig. 2.1 Map of Okinawa Main Island indicating USFJ facilities. (Source: U.S. military facilities and areas on Okinawa main island and its vicinity, Okinawa Prefectural Government, Washington, DC Office) 24

Fig. 6.1 Relationship between the Ministry of Defence and the LMO/IAA. (Source: http://www.lmo.go.jp/english/purpose/index.html) 88

Fig. 6.2 Status of USFJ employees. (Source: USFJ Employment Guide 2018, page 4: https://www.lmo.go.jp/recruitment/pdf/pamphlet_en.pdf) 89

List of Tables

Table 3.1	Base workers' wages in U.S. dollars	47
Table 3.2	Base Workers' Wages in B-yen	47
Table 6.1	Number of USFJ employees and retirees (ten-year overview, 2008–2017)	90

CHAPTER 1

Behind the Barbed Wire Fence

"Now I had to go to the U.S. Embassy to apply for a visa just to return to my old home," Raphael Miyagi[1] told me one autumn day in September 2007. We were seated at a doughnut shop inside a shopping mall in Naha, the Okinawan capital, where I talked to him about his life in Okinawa and the Philippines as well as his work on one of the U.S. bases in the prefecture. Raphael, at that time, was in his 50s, and has been living in Okinawa for around 30 years. Despite this, we spoke in both English and Filipino (Tagalog) interspersed with some Japanese words and expressions. His "old home", as it turns out, is Okinawa—the place where he was born and his mother's place of origin.

Up until 1972, Okinawa was governed by the American Occupation Forces and this was the Okinawa Raphael was born in and returned to, a year before its reversion to Japan. This was a turning point in his life, when at the young age of 20, he set out to travel from Manila to Okinawa for a supposedly short visit: a visit though that saw him staying in the southernmost Japanese prefecture for 40 years and counting. He was in his second year of studies at a university in Manila when he decided to make the trip in October 1971. Classes in Manila were suspended a number of times due to protests and rallies against the government of then President Ferdinand Marcos, who declared martial law the following year in 1972.

When Raphael arrived in Okinawa, he was surprised to find out that there were a lot of work opportunities there, particularly inside the U.S. military bases, dotting the main island. Trying his luck in landing a job, he found himself starting work for the U.S. military as a civilian employee at Camp Kinser in Urasoe City, a few kilometres north of Naha. This was on 3 January 1972, a mere three months after his arrival in 1971. Upon moving to the Philippines 15 years prior to his return to the place of his birth, Raphael lost whatever Japanese language he learned when he was attending primary school in Okinawa. Thus, working on these military installations was the best option for him as he need not know Japanese to land a job inside the U.S. bases.

Raphael was born in Koza City, now known as Okinawa City, in the central part of the main island of Okinawa prefecture, in December 1950. His Filipino father was working with the U.S. military, when he met and married an Okinawan woman—Raphael's mother—in Okinawa. Spending the early years of his childhood in Okinawa, he and his whole family had to move to his father's country upon the termination of his father's work contract. As it turns out, the experience of Raphael was not particular to his family. It was also the experience shared by countless others.

Meanwhile, five years after Raphael returned to his birthplace, Marco Yara decided to return to Okinawa in 1976. I first met Marco at Oroku Catholic Church in Naha in March 2010 after the 10 a.m. Sunday Mass and he gladly talked to me about his life as well as his own experiences of growing up in Okinawa. We were seated at a food court of a shopping centre in Naha's Shintoshin district, which in Japanese translates to "new metropolitan centre", a district that used to be the location of the U.S. Military Makiminato Housing District (*Beigun Makiminato Jūtaku Chiku*) from the early 1950s until it was returned in 1987. Marco mentioned to me that he was a college student in the Philippines when he decided on the return trip to the land of his birth mainly because of the unstable political situation in the Philippines, which was under martial rule during the Marcos regime. Upon his arrival in Okinawa, he decided to look for work and engaged himself in different jobs before landing in his present job (at the time of interview) at Futenma Air Base, a U.S. military facility located in the middle of Ginowan City, several kilometres north of Naha, in 1989.

Marco was born in a town called Akamichi (which was under Gushikawa City, and is now known as Uruma City), located near Koza City, and grew up in the Moromi district in Koza. Like Raphael, his father was also a Filipino who worked in a U.S. base facility in Okinawa as a heavy equipment operator. There, his father met and married his Okinawan mother. Spending the early years of his life in Okinawa attending an international school, Marco experienced difficulty understanding the lectures as he used to speak Japanese at home. His Filipino name also prompted him to question who and what he really was: "*Pumasok ako [nang] hindi ko alam kung ano ako—Pilipino ba ako o ano? Bakit ako may pangalan na ganito?* (I went to school, not knowing what I was—am I Filipino or what? Why do I have a name like this?)". These questions were momentarily put to a halt when Marco moved to the Philippines with his family when he was in the second grade of elementary school. The move to the Philippines was prompted by the expiration of his father's work contract.

A decade after Marco's return to Okinawa, Stephanie Ojana decided to take the same route and return to her birthplace. I met and spoke to Stephanie, then in her 50s, at a Japanese restaurant inside a shopping mall across Kadena Airbase, on a warm early autumn day back in September 2007. She told me that after working for 11 years in an insurance company in the Philippines, she decided to return to Okinawa in February 1986 and acquire Japanese nationality. Like Raphael and Marco, Stephanie was born in Okinawa to a Filipino father who was a civilian employee on base during the American Occupation, while her mother is Okinawan. Leaving Okinawa for the Philippines with her family in 1961 at the young age of five, Stephanie barely remembered her Japanese upon her return to island in the late 1980s. Like Raphael and Marco's fathers, Stephanie's father was also working on a contractual basis and had to return to the Philippines upon the contract's expiry.

It was in January 1987 that Stephanie found work in Okinawa as an editor for the air force's and marine's newspapers. However, after four and a half years of working as an editor, she quit her job and went to the mainland to work for Sony, where she worked as a contract worker for six months. Before finally settling in Okinawa in 1999, she had travelled back and forth between Okinawa and the Japanese mainland a number of times. Currently retired, she was working as a shift manager for a fast-food outlet at Kadena Air Base when I met her. Kadena Air Base is the largest air force installation in the Asia-Pacific region, which spans a huge area covering the towns of Kadena and Chatan, and Okinawa City.

On my visits and temporary sojourn in Okinawa from 2007 to 2013, as well as my sporadic trips there from 2014 to 2018, I met and spoke with people like Raphael, Marco, and Stephanie who all share the same life histories—their birth in Okinawa to an Okinawan mother and a Filipino father, their move to the Philippines in their childhood, their return to their birthplace in their adult years, the acquisition of a Japanese nationality, their base-related work, their families in Okinawa—and probably, the same futures. I met them in churches (both Catholic and Protestant), in parties hosted by Filipino organizations in Okinawa, at the Philippine Honorary Consulate, as well as on- and off-base. The exact population of this particular group is difficult to grasp due to the fact that most of them have acquired Japanese nationality and Japanese census data do not necessarily indicate a person's ethnic background, much less his/her parentage. As with convention, they have Japanese names that they use in formal settings and in official documents (although some chose to retain their Filipino/Western first names, writing them in *katakana*), but in social interactions among themselves, with non-Japanese, and with other Filipinos (including myself), they tend to use their Filipino/Western first names or even nicknames. Do I consider them Japanese or Okinawan? Or Filipino? Why do most of them work on base, or do work related to the U.S. military? These were some of the many questions I tried to answer when I first met these individuals more than a decade ago. Many were answered in the course of my research, and many more questions came up, especially those pertaining to the future—an uncertainty that these people, not even I, can fully prepare for.

The above vignettes of Raphael, Marco, and Stephanie are just few of the many accounts of civilians working (or have worked) on U.S. military bases in Okinawa and in other parts of East Asia. The existence of these individuals is oftentimes overlooked as much focus is accorded to the more conspicuous U.S. military troops that are assigned for duty on these bases. Base towns and communities surrounding these military installations are wont to the ubiquitous presence of these military personnel that they have become part of the socio-cultural landscape of these communities. However, the civilian workforce on base—Third Country Nationals (TCNs) and so-called Local Nationals (LNs)—seems to be "invisible" as if escaping the people's consciousness. Nevertheless, it cannot be denied that civilian workers occupy a large part of the manpower that supports the existence of these military installations for the purposes they are supposed to serve. These workers have been crucial since the early stages of base construction as they provided cheap and temporary labour. Both locals (LNs) and people from other countries (TCNs) were hired for these jobs; and this demand for labour—both for the construction and the day-to-day functioning of these bases—as well as the manner of hiring still continues up to the present day.

The Okinawan case, however, is worthy of note. It is common knowledge that the Government of Japan largely subsidizes the basing of the U.S. troops in the country as well as provides the necessary civilian workforce to support the U.S. military. Currently, most of the civilian workforce are Japanese nationals, with a significant number of them individuals having both Philippine and Okinawan parentage, and who work on a variety of jobs—from the professionally skilled class to those who are engaged in semi-skilled work. A large number of them are "returnees"—like Raphael, Marco, and Stephanie—who returned to their birthplace for a variety of reasons and managed to secure jobs on base. They call themselves Nisei or second generation in the Japanese language, emphasizing both their Philippine and Okinawan heritage.

This book is about the presence of this group of individuals that is usually hidden from the public's gaze and who live their lives between the U.S. military bases and Okinawan society. I shed light on the migrations that occurred between Okinawa and the Philippines during the immediate post-war years and the significant role that the United States Occupation Government in Japan played in this regard. Here, I note how transnational movements within East Asia during the Occupation period brought forth foreign workers to the Japanese archipelago, many of them from Asia, with most coming from the Philippines, to work on these bases. Currently, "remnants" of the foreign presence among base workers in the post-war era continue in contemporary base employment, albeit deemed "invisible".

I also examine the creation of a second generation of base workers, this time working (or have worked) under the Government of Japan, as well as their role—albeit passive—in the promotion of security in the region under the U.S.-Japan Security Treaty. Not overlooking agency in my discussions, I seek out their stories to illuminate issues of identity and belongingness that are part and parcel of the experience of migration. While nation-states still hold their significance in issues of migration, I also look at other factors such as social and kinship networks in the decision to migrate or return.

In this book, I first point to macro-level factors that enabled these migrations between Okinawa and the Philippines that started in the immediate post-war years, situating them within the context of the U.S. Military Occupation of Okinawa from 1945 to 1972, which I argue, still continues to this day owing to the U.S. military presence in the prefecture. While most literature attribute the migration to Japan of third-world nationals and the *Nikkeijin* or people of Japanese descent to economic factors linked to structural inequalities between and among states in the prevailing world system, I argue that migrations such as this particular one between Okinawa and the Philippines that started in the immediate post-war period and continue up to this day are also triggered by continuing U.S. hegemony in the region and the need to perpetuate this status quo. It should be noted that the United States has the largest number of military bases outside their country. I also point out that while economic factors indeed play important roles in problematizing South-North migration, socio-political and geopolitical, as well as other structural factors, are not less significant in this particular case.

Migrations and the U.S. Bases in Okinawa

Several cases of post-war out-migrations from Okinawa can be said to be linked to the occupation of the prefecture in the immediate post-war years. The U.S. Occupation Government worked to strengthen the militarization of Okinawa by increasing the number of military bases on the island. This was in response to the need to secure the U.S. military's strategic position in Okinawa, in the early years of the Cold War (Iacobelli 2017: 75–77). With this, the construction of U.S. bases necessitated the use of land owned by locals and most of them experienced having their land seized. Many of these Okinawans were also relocated to Bolivia (Amemiya 1996; Amemiya 2006) for this purpose. This emigration programme was carried out with the involvement of the Government of the Ryukyu Islands (GRI),[2] the local civilian government during the U.S. Occupation of Okinawa (Iacobelli 2017: 136–137). With the necessity for land on which to construct the bases, the need for labour becomes paramount; and it is not only the locals' labour that was sought for the construction of these military installations, but foreign nationals' as well, such as the Chinese and Filipinos. A large number of these foreign nationals—known as Third Country Nationals or TCNs—were Filipinos, recruited not only for the construction of these military installations but also to provide semi-skilled work as well as professional services to ensure the running and the maintenance of these bases. Alongside TCNs are LNs or local nationals, comprised of the local Okinawan population who were relegated to less skilled and unskilled labour. The existing hierarchies of race, ethnicity, nationalities, and genders that reflected post-war global hierarchies during that period were apparent in the hiring of this workforce that only served to reinforce these inequalities within base work. With this, I argue that work on base at that time was racialized and hierarchical; and for the TCNs who were on work contracts, base work—while financially rewarding—was also a source of uncertainty; especially among those who lacked capital—economic, cultural, and social—and those who decided to have their own families in Okinawa, such as Filipino men.

A large number of these Filipino male TCNs married Okinawan women. Several decades later, their offspring, the Nisei or the second generation (hereunto referred as Nisei[3]), began working on these military bases, reminiscent of their Filipino fathers from the late 1940s to the 1950s. While seemingly a reproduction of temporary base labour by the second generation, the Nisei are able to make capital work for them and they are not necessarily faced with the uncertainties that their fathers had during the immediate post-war years.

Meanwhile, the continuing presence of the U.S. bases in Okinawa and the increased presence of U.S. troops, ships, and planes in Philippine military bases under the Enhanced Defence Cooperation Agreement or EDCA,[4] signed in 2014 (Vitug 2018: 110–111), seem to attest that Okinawa and the Philippines are still seen as strategic areas by the United States. Japan's "subordinated" position as a "client state" (McCormack 2007) of the United States, where around 70 per cent of the country's U.S. military installations are concentrated on the main island of Okinawa, making it a "military colony" (Yoshida 2007; McCormack 2007: 156) in the literal sense of the word, as well as the post-colonial ties the world's largest superpower has with the Philippines, just goes to show that Asia has been and still continues to be "a site of U.S. expansion" (Espiritu 2008: 5).

Several conditions enabled the migrations between Okinawa and the Philippines during the immediate post-war years. These are: (1) the demand for labour, particularly for the construction of bases, as well as the need for base employees; (2) the need for people to address the needs of the U.S. military and their families, which includes teachers to address the educational needs of their children, entertainers, and service industry workers such as hotel and restaurant staff.

As a heuristic in understanding these migrations, I also indicate here the significance of the military base as a vantage point to understand and problematize these types of migrations. As a site for the various movements of military troops, workers and labour force, consumer goods (post-exchange or PX goods), information, and other services, I see the military bases in Okinawa as playing significant roles in the migrations of not only human resources, but also the circulation of capital—in this case mostly economic—that not necessarily translates to economic gains at the prefectural level, but rather works to create a class of individuals that are able to accumulate resources giving them more opportunities for social mobility. The bases also played a significant role in the creation of particular ethnic groups: the Amerasian, or the offspring of American servicemen and Okinawan women, and this particular group that this book talks about—the offspring of Filipino base workers and Okinawan women, which I consider the "Other" to the Amerasian. These individuals traverse two cultures—Filipino and Okinawan—an ethnic identity that served and serves as a passport for greater mobility, both economic and social. I also argue here that it is also due to the bases' economic value as a worksite, with the presence of jobs within these military installations that enabled the return migration of this group of individuals.

Military Bases and Civilian Workers

The presence of U.S. bases in a particular place is more often than not, equated with the existence of the U.S. military, the crimes they commit, the accidents that occur due to recklessness or to incidents involving aircraft crashes and the like, noise pollution, and minor altercations with locals living near the vicinity of these bases. In the case of Japan and South Korea, two places in East Asia that host most of these military installations in the region (the Philippines, of course had hosted what was the largest naval base in the region—the Subic Bay Naval Base—before the U.S. military was ousted from Philippine soil), these have become almost daily occurrences that base towns live with. However, notice is rarely given to civilian workers who make their livelihood inside these U.S. military bases, and who along with the military, may be seen to be instrumental in the functioning of these bases for the purposes they supposedly serve. Here, I take up the case of Okinawa, which hosts majority of all the U.S. military installations that are in the country, and examine the migration of civilian workers to this small southernmost island of the Japanese archipelago. The continued presence of the U.S. military bases in East Asia and more so in Okinawa, heeds the continuing call for people to take on skilled as well as semi-skilled jobs on base, either as directly hired employees or those working for companies (such as construction companies) that are contracted to work on these military installations. These civilian workers hired by the Government of Japan (under the Ministry of Defence) comprise the United States Forces of Japan (USFJ) employees hired in accordance with the U.S.-Japan Security Treaty. Most of these USFJ employees are Japanese nationals, with a significant number of them having both Philippine and Okinawan parentage.

While studies on the movements of peoples within East Asia (Northeast and Southeast) abound, studies specifically looking at migrations in the context of military basing in the region are not. Moreover, those studies focusing on civilian workers on these military installations are scant. This book attempts to address this lack in scholarship on civilian workers on U.S. military bases by looking at civilian workers hired to work as TCNs during the Occupation of Okinawa, as well as the current presence of contemporary civilian base workers known as USFJ employees. The data I use here are based on life stories culled from semi-structured interviews I had with USFJ employees from 2007 to 2010, as well as follow-up interviews and conversations I had with them sporadically from 2012 to 2018. I also utilize archival data, mostly declassified documents from the United States Civil Administration of the Ryukyus or USCAR, to re-create these migrations that occurred in these military bases during the Occupation Period.

This group of base workers has had a significant history than their local (Okinawan) counterparts, as their migration histories and processes, I argue, are linked to both these places' relationships with the United States of America; that is, the Philippines' role as an erstwhile colony and Okinawa's history of American Occupation from 1945–1972—which ended 20 more years after that of the Japanese mainland—as well as its position as host to three-fourths of the total number of U.S. bases in Japan, which I argue to be related to the "imperialistic activity" (Go 2008: 8) of the U.S. as attested to by the continued presence—in the post-Cold War years—of the largest number of U.S. troops in East Asia in this small island alone.

Born in Okinawa and moving to the Philippines in their childhood and adolescent years, these Nisei made the return trip back to their birthplace for a variety of reasons. Nevertheless, in examining the return movement of these individuals, the role of the United States and its current presence in the East Asian region particularly in Okinawa is a very crucial one and thus a significant part in this whole migration project.

Several factors for the return of these Nisei to Okinawa can be mentioned here. Aside from evident reasons such as financial and job stability, other main reasons for the return include the acquisition of Japanese nationality as well as the desire to connect with one's Okinawan roots.

Some, like Raphael and Marco, made the return trip due to socio-political conditions in the Philippines when they were young adults. Other reasons include marriage, further studies, and professional training. Some of these Nisei returned with their families, yet others returned as individual returnees. The return movement started as early as the 1970s, when some Nisei began working as civilian workers on U.S. military installations in Okinawa.

RETURN AND THE NISEI

Return migration, particularly ethnic return migration—be it temporary or permanent—such as that of the Latin American *Nikkeijin*, is more often than not viewed within the context of the host countries' demand for labour and people to take on unskilled work that their nationals do not want (Tsuda 2003), ethnic nationalism (Joppke 2005), and economic and financial policies of the host government usually in the guise of investment opportunities offered to these returnees (such as the *balikbayan* or "returnee" programme in the Philippines which started in the 1970s during the Marcos regime). Most of these studies though focus on an "ethnically homogeneous" group of people returning to the "homeland". The Nisei however challenge this dominant discourse on return migration. Having both Okinawan and Philippine parentage, the Nisei shatter the common perception of return migrants as coming from a homogeneous group or sharing a similar ethnicity.

This work, which looks at the return migration of the Nisei and base work in Okinawa, can be said to be a pioneering one as studies focusing on people with both Philippine and Okinawan parentage are rare. While the Philippine *Nikkeijin* (Filipinos of Japanese descent) and the Brazilian *Nikkeijin* (Brazilians of Japanese descent) and their return migration to Japan have been studied by some researchers (Iijima and Ohno 2010; Ohno and Iijima 2010; Tsuda 2003, 2009), studies that focus solely on people of Okinawan descent are seldom seen. Moreover, the existence itself of this group of Nisei with Philippine and Okinawan parentage, has been accorded very little notice in academic research, and in most instances, they are subsumed under the category of *Nikkeijin* or the Philippine *Nikkeijin*. To do so, I believe, would undervalue the separate histories and the distinct identity formations of this particular group. Due primarily to their having a significant history that can be traced back to the erstwhile Kingdom of the Ryukyus, as well as a unique cultural identity, lumping the Okinawans together with the mainland Japanese is tantamount to undermining their existence as distinct individuals with their own migration stories. Moreover, the U.S. Occupation of Okinawa plays a significant role in these people's lives since Okinawans during that time were not Japanese nationals, nor were they considered U.S. nationals. Their citizenship though was administered by the U.S. Occupation Government at that time. The stories then that these Nisei tell are intertwined with the historical ties—post-war ties, in particular—Okinawa and the Philippines have shared and continue to share.

While the concept of return has been problematized in migration literature and current debates on the permanency and the temporariness of the return process have brought up several issues that need to be further studied (Cassarino 2004; Suzuki 2010; Boccagni 2017), I use the word return here not only to point to the Nisei's movement back to their place of birth but also how these individuals described their move to Okinawa—whether they describe this as a move back, a going back, or a return.

Return also implies an ambiguity in movement and a return (migration) may not necessarily indicate permanence, but rather a temporariness or a transitoriness, which I further explore in the succeeding chapters. This ambiguity, I argue, is due to the following:

1. In the case of Latin Americans and/or Americans (particularly Hawaiians) of Okinawan descent residing in Okinawa, many of these individuals were born outside Okinawa, and thus the notion of Okinawa as a "homeland", much less of a birthplace, is inapplicable in this sense. While the "return" to a "homeland" may actually point to or connote a return to an ancestral homeland, or the birthplace of their parents, for most of these individuals, this "homeland" is only a distant and an imagined one.
2. In the case of the Nisei, who are born to an Okinawan mother and a Filipino father, their birth in Okinawa before moving to the Philippines in their adolescent years and their eventual move to Okinawa for work, seems to qualify them as returnees. They are in effect returning to their place of birth. However, these Nisei only spent several years of their lives in Okinawa, and moved to the Philippines with their families as children, with many of them spending quite a number of years there, only to return to Okinawa as an adult. Moreover, these Nisei have both Okinawan and Philippine ancestry (dual ancestry). Therefore, strictly speaking, it can be said that their "home", "ancestral land (*sokoku*)" or "homeland (*kokyō*)"

are both Okinawa and the Philippines.[5] As I previously mentioned, most literature on return migration presuppose an ethnically homogeneous group of people returning to the "homeland". The Nisei, having both Okinawan and Philippine ancestry, challenges this dominant discourse regarding ethnic return migration.

Moreover, while it can be said that the concept of return indicates the idea of a "return home", or of "returning to one's origins", I also argue here that return for the Nisei is transitory and that for them, where and what home is, are defined according to how they construct their identity/ies in relation to current global conditions.

For the Nisei, their return to Okinawa and their work as civilian workers on U.S. military bases place them in an ambivalent position vis-à-vis Okinawan society, which was their birthplace, but now seems to function as a "host society" as well. Their nationality as Japanese categorizes them as such, however their insufficient knowledge of the language (particularly in reading and writing) puts them in a position of being outside, and hence they are more often than not, regarded as foreigners, as they are seen as a cultural "Other". The above being said, perceptions of home, I argue, should not be seen as fixed and an end in itself, and return should not be seen as a one-way route to a fixed destination (i.e. the "return home"). Rather, home for these Nisei should be seen as a situational construct and the return should be seen as the process by which they negotiate their idea of "routes" and "roots" (Clifford 1994, 1997) and the process by which they construct their home. I elaborate more on these issues in the succeeding chapters.

Capital, Networks, and Transnational Identities

As the title states, this work is about *Transnational Identities on Okinawa's Military Bases*—primarily those who are engaged in civilian work on military bases scattered throughout the main island of Okinawa. They are "invisible armies", since discussions about military basing are usually equated with military troops stationed in these base towns or host cities. Much like military troops, these civilian workers—whether TCNs, LNs, or USFJ employees—play significant roles in military basing.

Throughout this book, I argue that the U.S. Military Occupation of Okinawa needs to be considered as a transnational project that not only involves the U.S. and Japanese governments, but also other governments deemed "peripheral" in this whole scheme, such as the Philippines. I earlier stated that TCNs were hired to work on the construction and the staffing of these U.S. military bases during the immediate post-war years, and that most of them were Filipino nationals, and were male. While stationed in Okinawa, these Filipinos married (some co-habited) local women, producing "half-Filipino" and "half-Okinawan" offspring—a product of military occupation in the Japanese prefecture. These offspring, referred throughout this work as Nisei, comprise an ethnic group that is characteristic of so-called transnational identities, particularly in problematizing their migration process/es as well as return, which also informs and shapes their perceptions of what and where home is. Meanwhile, in this whole migration scheme, the significant role that capital and networks play cannot be denied.

Here, I primarily use the concepts of cultural, economic, and social capital (Bourdieu 1926) to illustrate how the return migration of the Nisei to Okinawa was made possible. Economic capital points to anything that can easily be converted into money such as property, wealth, and income. Cultural capital, meanwhile, can also be converted into economic capital and is institutionalized in the form of academic and educational qualifications. Here, Pierre Bourdieu also points out to the embodied and objectified state of cultural capital, in the form of "dispositions of the mind and body" and "taste" for the former, and cultural or material goods (indicating one's social class) for the latter (Ibid). Lastly, social capital points to "social obligations" or "connections" (Ibid).

The Nisei's Okinawan ethnicity due to their part-Okinawan parentage also works as a form of cultural capital. My reference to ethnicity throughout this study is based on Max Weber's definition of ethnic groups, which are those groups that have a "memory" of a shared past that may be due to migration. Weber states that if this memory (of migration) remains alive, there exists a "very specific and often extremely powerful sense of ethnic identity" (Weber 1968: 390). Meanwhile, taking off from Fredrik Barth's (1969) assertion that self-ascription and ascription by others are important in the creation of ethnic groups, and that ethnic identity functions not only as a marker for the group, but more as a boundary to exclude other groups, I discuss in Chap. 4 how "Japanese" and "half" are both ascribed and self-ascribed identities, and how each of these two categories delineate "boundaries" and hence engage in "boundary making process/es".

The Nisei's transnational identities may also be seen to influence their future trajectories, that is life after working as USFJ employees. These future trajectories are not only tied to familial relationships, but also to socio-cultural and politico-economic factors, such as the bases' continued existence in Okinawa in the years to come.

THE RESEARCH

For this work, I focus on eight life stories of Nisei USFJ employees (current and former) as well as include my informal conversations with other Nisei base workers who I encountered at Oroku Catholic Church in Naha, in parties hosted by the FILCOMRI (Filipino Community of the Ryukyu Islands) and AFILJAN (Association of Filipino Japanese Nationals). Oroku Catholic Church is significant due to the presence of the Nisei and their *issei* (first generation in Japanese,) mothers, where an estimated 90 per cent of "Filipino" parishioners in this Church are actually Nisei. I also include here the non-base worker Nisei who I encountered during my fieldwork. I interviewed these Nisei in Naha City, Kita Nakagusuku Village, Okinawa City, Chatan Town, and Ginowan City—the latter three cities are currently host to some U.S. bases, such as the Futenma Airbase (in Ginowan) and the Kadena Airbase, which occupies a large area spanning Okinawa City, Chatan Town, and Kita Nakagusuku Village. Naha used to host the Naha Air Base during the American Occupation; currently the facility is used by the Japan Air Self-Defence Forces and is officially called the *Kōkū Jieitai Naha Kichi* (Naha Air Base) and is located within Naha Airport. The interviews were conducted in English, Tagalog, and Taglish (which is a mixture of Tagalog and English), with some Japanese words interspersed throughout the conversations.

In the course of fieldwork in 2012–2013, I also met Filipino veteran TCNs who have made Okinawa their home. Two of them gladly shared their stories with me and these give a human face to discussions on the hiring of Filipino workers during the American Occupation of Okinawa in the immediate post-war years. Their stories confirmed the historical and archival data I collected from the Okinawa Prefectural Archives at Haebaru-cho, which I used to re-construct and analyse the migrations that occurred between Okinawa and the Philippines during the U.S. Occupation of the prefecture as well as several issues pertaining to this particular migration.

Migrant narratives of home and migration do not only serve to weave theory into the migrant experience, but also pose a challenge to the researcher who "re-narrates" these stories in an attempt to understand and interpret the migration phenomena. I addressed this methodological issue when I wrote and analysed these people's narratives.

ORGANIZATION OF THE BOOK

This book is mainly about the civilian population working on U.S. bases in Okinawa, Japan, as employees of the United States Forces in Japan, and are mainly employed by the Ministry of Defence of the Japanese Government to assist in carrying out the aims of the U.S.-Japan Security Treaty. With the current territorial disputes and geopolitical tensions in the Asia-Pacific region, such as the North Korean threat and the Chinese encroachment on several island possessions in the South China Sea, the region has become more and more significant not only in terms of security, but also with regards to the mobilization and movement not only of military personnel, but also of other human resources (such as civilian workers), as well as consumer goods, capital, information, and services. Okinawa is an interesting case study, as its strategic position in East Asia is deemed to have great importance concerning security issues in the region. Rather than focus on political and security issues and the role of the military, this book will give notice to the thousands of civilian employees working on these U.S. bases in Okinawa, as they also play a valuable role in the maintenance and functioning of these military installations as well as in assisting the military troops stationed in the region. Here, I look at a particular group of base workers that, I argue, was created by the U.S. Military Occupation of Okinawa—a second generation of base workers who considered base work as a vehicle for socio-economic mobility, and for many of them, was also a reason for their return to the land of their birth.

As a background to the remarkable presence of the U.S. military on the island of Okinawa, I explore the reason for the geopolitical significance of this southern Japanese archipelago in *Chap. 2: Military Bases in East Asia: The Case of Okinawa*, where I closely look at the case of Okinawa, which holds the most number of U.S. bases in East Asia (both Northeast and Southeast Asia). I start the chapter with a short historical background of the events that led to the American Occupation of Japan and Okinawa. This chapter provides a historical context to the book to familiarize readers who may not be well-versed about the American Occupation of Japan and Okinawa and how the main island of Okinawa prefecture came to host around 70 per cent of the U.S. military bases in the country.

Chapter 3: Transnational Movements During the Occupation of Okinawa: Third Country Nationals and the U.S. Bases situates the Occupation of Okinawa in a transnational context by looking at transnational movements of people, goods, information, and such not only between the United States and Japan/Okinawa, but in a more regional (i.e. Asia-Pacific) context. Here, I argue that the Occupation of Okinawa should also be regarded as a transnational project that involved actors other than the U.S. and the Japanese governments. In this chapter, I focus on what could be argued as the least looked-at actor in military basing—civilian base workers. During the immediate post-war years, Third Country Nationals or TCNs came from various countries such as India, China, and the Philippines.

There was a significant number of intermarriages among TCNs and Okinawan women during the immediate post-war years. These unions produced children that are considered "half" or "hāfu" in the Japanese parlance. *Chapter 4: The "Other" Mixed Race: The Nisei in Perspective* discusses the creation of a group of individuals due in part to the migrations that occurred in the context of military basing in Okinawa. These individuals are the "Other" to the Amerasian—offspring of American servicemen stationed in Asia and Asian women. In this chapter, I point to the significance of these groups' existence since the immediate post-war years, as challenging the concepts of racial and ethnic "purity" in Japan and Okinawa. I also give a short discussion on the Amerasian and link and compare this group with the half-Filipino and half-Okinawan offspring of these TCNs and Okinawan women. Moreover, I provide a micro-level discussion of the identity formation of these Nisei. This chapter focuses on the birth of the Nisei in Okinawa and their early years there, and follows them when they moved to the Philippines during their childhood and adolescent years up until their decision to return to the land of their birth as adults.

Following the discussion on the Nisei's identity formation, *Chap. 5: The Return to Okinawa: Capital, Networks, Mobility,* looks at the return of these Nisei to Okinawa, their birthplace, after spending much of their adolescent and early adult lives in the Philippines. This chapter explores the causes, motivations, and reasons for the return, and emphasizes that most of these Nisei returned to work as United States Forces in Japan employees in U.S. military bases on the main island of Okinawa. I also indicate here the role of ethnicity as cultural capital in the return migration process as well as in the eventual acquisition of Japanese nationality, which is not only linked to their Okinawan parentage, but also to nationality rules during the period that enabled children born out of wedlock to take on the nationality of their mothers rather than their fathers'.

In Chap. 5, I discuss how return and the acquisition of Japanese nationality is largely instrumental and motivated by capital accumulation. Furthermore, the Nisei's proficiency and fluency in the English language enabled them to land in coveted base jobs, which translated into economic and social mobility, as opposed to non-Filipino returnees of Okinawan descent, who had to settle for semi-skilled and low-skilled work outside the bases due to their limited English and Japanese abilities. I argue that for the Nisei, base work is also a means for them to locate their place within Okinawan society, as their Japanese linguistic handicap limits them from (full) participation in economic processes as they would only be relegated to unskilled work if it were not for the availability of jobs on these military bases.

Chapter 6: The Other Army: United States Forces in Japan Employees in Okinawa gives an overview of the hiring of United States Forces in Japan employees or USFJ employees through the Labour Management Organization for USFJ employees or LMO. According to the LMO, USFJ employees are employees "who are hired by the Government of Japan (Ministry of Defence) for the purpose of accomplishing the mission of the USFJ and work on the USFJ facilities" (LMO/IAA website). Here, I give a background about the agency and its relationship with the Ministry of Defence, the relevance of employing these workers, the different types of work contracts available for jobs on base, as well as statistical data regarding base employment not only on Okinawan bases but also in other regions of Japan that host U.S. military installations.

Chapter 7: "Home Is where the Heart Is?" An Invisible Minority looks at perceptions of where and what home is for these returnees. The return of the Nisei can be situated in a socio-cultural and historical context and in this chapter, I illustrate how perceptions of home among these Nisei base employees are also shaped by these structural factors. Here, I look at the idea of an "invisible minority" and how these second-generation base workers could be said to be "invisible" as their existence and their plight is not visibly recognized unlike other "foreign" groups. Due to their Japanese nationality, they are legally Japanese, but culturally, they are not seen as such. They can be considered to be a "minority within a minority"; a group of Japanese nationals who are not "culturally" Japanese, thus challenging notions of what being Japanese (or Okinawan) is. Furthermore, I emphasize here that military basing has engendered migrations in the region, at the same time creating a new category of half-Japanese or half-Okinawan individuals that make up a large percentage of USFJ employees. While their nationality as Japanese does not define them as foreign, their return to Okinawa to work on these bases, as well as issues regarding linguistic and cultural differences, and social integration seemingly regard their presence as similar to that of migrants, thus belying their status as Japanese.

The concluding chapter, *Chap. 8: Future Trajectories: A Conclusion*, ends the book by asking what is in store for the future of base work in Okinawa. First, I look at where these USFJ employees are now, and how they are spending their retirement years, or their plans for retirement. I also look at the future in store for civilian workers in military bases in the case of base closures, or in case of changes in the Security Treaty between the United States and Japan. The existence of military bases in Japan and the Asia-Pacific region, while believed to provide security in the region and is a source of employment among the local populace, also invites other contentious issues such as environmental problems, noise pollution, crimes, accidents, and others.

I end this book by pointing out the significance of looking within the walls of these bases to give attention to civilian base employees and the significant roles they play in the functioning of these military installations, as well as the importance of listening to their voices as they are also part of the whole scheme of military basing in the region.

Notes

1. All names appearing here are pseudonyms.
2. The Government of the Ryukyu Islands (GRI) or *Ryūkyū Seifu*, was created by the United States Civil Administration of the Ryukyus (USCAR) in April 1952 and was abolished when Okinawa was reverted to the Japanese mainland in 1972.
3. Throughout the book, I capitalize the first letter of Nisei, to indicate it as an identity marker used by these individuals. I discuss more about the Nisei identity in Chap. 4.

4. The Enhanced Defence Cooperation Agreement or EDCA was a successor to the Visiting Forces Agreement or VFA, and was signed in 2014, to address the need for heightened defence measures within the context of the South China Sea disputes. There were debates as to the ratification of the EDCA, but the Supreme Court of the Philippines ruled in favour of ratifying the agreement. (See Vitug 2018: 110–112)
5. Needless to say, there are Nisei who were born in the Philippines and are now working and residing in Okinawa.

References

Amemiya, K. (1996, October 25). The Bolivian Connection: U.S. Bases and Okinawan Emigration. *Japan Policy Research Institute Working Paper no. 25.* http://www.jpri.org/publications/workingpapers/wp25.html. Accessed 10 Oct 2018.

Amemiya, K. (2006). Four Governments and a New Land: Emigration to Bolivia. In N. Adachi (Ed.), *Japanese Diasporas: Unsung Pasts, Conflicting Presents, and Uncertain Futures* (pp. 175–190). London: Routledge.

Barth, F. (1969). *Ethnic Groups and Boundaries: The Social Organization of Culture and Difference.* Boston: Little Brown.

Boccagni, P. (2017). *Migration and the Search for Home: Mapping Domestic Space in Migrants' Everyday Lives.* New York: Palgrave Macmillan.

Bourdieu, P. (1926). The Forms of Capital. In J. Richardson (Ed.), *Handbook of Theory of Research for the Sociology of Education* (pp. 46–58). New York: Greenwood Press.

Cassarino, J. P. (2004). Theorising Return Migration: The Conceptual Approach to Return Migrants Revisited. *International Journal on Multicultural Societies, 6*(2), 253–279.

Clifford, J. (1994). Diasporas. *Cultural Anthropology, 9*(3), 302–338.

Clifford, J. (1997). *Routes: Travel and Translation in the Late Twentieth Century.* Cambridge: Harvard University Press.

Espiritu, Y. L. (2008). *Homebound: Filipino American Lives Across Cultures, Communities, and Countries* (Philippine ed.). Quezon City: Ateneo de Manila University Press.

Go, J. (2008). *American Empire and the Politics of Meaning: Elite Political Cultures in the Philippines and Puerto Rico during U.S. Colonialism* (Philippine ed.). Quezon City: Ateneo de Manila University Press.

Iacobelli, P. (2017). *Postwar Emigration to South America from Japan and the Ryukyu Islands.* London: Bloomsbury Academic Press.

Iijima, M., & Ohno, S. (2010). Firipin Nikkei 'Kikan' Imin no Seikatsu, Shiminken, Aidentiti: Shitsumonhyō ni yoru Zenkoku Jittai Chōsa Kekka wo Chōshin ni. *Bulletin of Kyushu University Asia Centre, 4,* 35–54.

Joppke, C. (2005). *Selecting by Origin: Ethnic Migration in the Liberal State.* Cambridge: Harvard University Press.
Labour Management Organization for USFJ Employees, Incorporated Administrative Agency (LMO/IAA) website. https://www.lmo.go.jp/. Accessed 1 Sept 2018.
McCormack, G. (2007). *Client State: Japan in the American Embrace.* London: Verso.
Ohno, S., & Iijima, M. (2010, June). *Nihon Zaijō Firipin Nikkeijin no Shiminken, Seikatsu, Aidentiti: Shitusmonhyō Haifu ni yoru Zenkoku Jittai Chōsa Hōkokusho (Citizenships, Lives, and Identities of the Philippine Nikkeijin Residing in Japan: Report on the Results of a Nationwide Questionnaire Survey).* Fukuoka: Kyushu University.
Suzuki, T. (2010). *Embodying Belonging: Racializing Okinawan Diaspora in Bolivia and Japan.* Honolulu: University of Hawaii Press.
Tsuda, T. (2003). *Strangers in the Ethnic Homeland: Japanese Brazilian Return Migration in Transnational Perspective.* New York: Columbia University Press.
Tsuda, T. (Ed.). (2009). *Diasporic Homecomings: Ethnic Return Migration in Comparative Perspective.* Stanford: Stanford University Press.
Vitug, M. D. (2018). *Rock Solid: How the Philippines Won its Maritime Case against China.* Quezon City: Ateneo de Manila University Press.
Weber, M. (1968). *Economy and Society: An Outline of Interpretive Sociology* (Vol. 1, G. Roth & C. Wittich Eds.). New York: Bedminton Press. https://www.ucpress.edu/book/9780520280021/economy-and-society.
Yoshida, K. (2007). *"Gunji Shokuminchi" Okinawa: Nihon Hondo to no "Ondosa" no Shōtai.* Tokyo: Kōbunken.

CHAPTER 2

Military Bases in East Asia: The Case of Okinawa

My visits to Okinawa saw me riding the bus along Highway 58 or National Route 58—an extensive road that stretches from the southern part of Kyushu Island in Kagoshima and extends to the island of Okinawa with its terminus at Naha, the capital city. Naha was my base while doing this study, and coming from this city, these bus trips usually took me north to other cities in the prefecture. As the bus traverses this highway, barbed-wire fences begin to appear on the left side of the road upon reaching the first city north of Naha, Urasoe City—home to Camp Kinser. A few kilometres ahead is Ginowan City, where the Marine Corps Air Station Futenma (MCAS Futenma) of Futenma Air Base is located. Futenma is currently making news due to the planned relocation of this facility to the north of the main island of Okinawa—Henoko, in Nago City—which has sparked numerous protests within the island and even in mainland Japan. Futenma Base is located right in the middle of Ginowan City and proponents for its relocation suggest doing so to avoid further accidents and noise pollution that are related to the presence of this military installation in the city. Those against relocation to the north of Okinawa argue on environmental grounds and wish to have the facility relocated to the Japanese mainland instead, which is not stipulated in the U.S.-Japan Agreement and to which the Japanese government would not readily agree to. The results of the February 2019 referendum showed a stunning 72 per cent of votes against the relocation of Futenma to Henoko, but the Abe administration seems to have decided to push through with its plans (*The Asahi Shimbun*, 25 February 2019).

© The Author(s) 2020
J. O. Zulueta, *Transnational Identities on Okinawa's Military Bases*,
https://doi.org/10.1007/978-981-32-9787-6_2

Further up north is Okinawa City, formerly known as Koza, which was a lively base town during the immediate post-war years. While the city may have lost its post-wartime atmosphere, remnants of base culture can still be seen in this now sleepy town in central Okinawa. I have been to Okinawa City a few times—both to meet my informants and to walk along the streets of the once-lively area of Koza that now merely hark of memories of American culture, jazz, the military, sex, and violence that are embedded in histories of riots (the Koza Riots), conflicts, and protests against the foreign occupier and its stronghold of military installations. Okinawa City currently hosts six U.S. military bases—Kadena Ammunition Storage Area, Camp Shields, Awase Communication Site, Camp Foster (formerly, Camp Zukeran), the Army Oil Storage Facility, and Kadena Airbase—the largest air base in the region, which also extends to the neighbouring towns of Kadena and Chatan.

The presence of the U.S. military on this tiny island cannot be ignored indeed. While the younger generation of Okinawans have become used to living side-by-side with these bases where U.S. servicemen and American cultural artefacts (such as fast food, post-exchange or PX goods) have become a ubiquitous sight, to the older generation these military bases signify encroachment on the land that their ancestors have lived on for centuries, as well as an attack on the people's sovereignty upon the decision to have Okinawa involuntarily host around 70 per cent of Japan's U.S. military bases (Defense of Japan Pamphlet, 2018).[1]

U.S. basing in East Asia occurred in conjunction with several geopolitical and socio-economic changes in the region since the post-war era leading up to the post-Cold War years. These changes precipitated the perceived need for security in the region to ward off threats to the status quo, and provide the necessary assistance to the existing militaries in the region in return for more active cooperation for the fight against imminent fears. In the following sections, I give the rationale for the creation of these military bases as well as a short history of Okinawa in the immediate post-war years and the beginnings of Okinawa's love and hate relationship with the U.S. presence in their midst.

Overseas Bases of the U.S. Military

Military bases are installations that "represent a confluence of labour (soldiers, paramilitary workers, and civilians), land, and capital in the form of static facilities, supplies, and equipment" (Lutz 2009: 4). The United

States so far, is the only country in the world that has a network of military bases globally. These military installations were built in order to "contain" the communist threat in the East Asian region during the Cold War years. These bases have existed (and continue to exist) to provide military protection to host countries and also to the so-called free world—pertaining largely to the countries that are allies of the United States (Iacobelli 2017: 258). Pedro Iacobelli (2018) also points to the significance of the Korean War (1950–1953) in the construction of military bases in Okinawa during this period. There was an influx of military personnel and "materials" to Okinawa from Korea during this time, thus transforming the Okinawan landscape (Iacobelli 2018: 110). Currently, these bases continue to exist under the guise of protection against threats of war and military aggression—such as the fight against Islamic fundamentalism and terrorism, notwithstanding the threat the Asia-Pacific region feels from the hermit state of North Korea and the rise of its neighbour, China. Critics of the U.S. bases and military presence throughout the world attribute the existence of these bases to the creation of an "empire", where a country exerts its political dominance on a region. Lutz adds that bases have been used to control the political and economic life of the host country, especially with regards to foreign policy (Lutz 2009: 8). It is not only the U.S. government, but also the military, and various corporations (especially construction companies) that benefit from the bases' continued existence (Fig. 2.1).

Chalmers Johnson writes that the United States' maintenance of its military bases overseas after the Cold War Period has five "missions": "1) maintaining absolute military preponderance over the rest of the world… ; 2) eavesdropping on the communications of citizens, allies, and enemies alike… ; 3) attempting to control as many sources of petroleum as possible… ; 4) providing work and income for the military-industrial complex… ; and 5) ensuring that members of the military and their families live comfortably and are well entertained while serving abroad" (Johnson 2004: 151–152). Johnson speaks of present-day American imperialism that is manifested though its network of military bases scattered throughout the world. By using the word, "missions", he indicates that the military bases exist to achieve a particular aim, and gathering from what he enumerated, it can be inferred that this aim points to America's present-day hegemonic interests. Moreover, the fourth and fifth "missions" above signify the presence of actors involved other than the U.S. military and their families, and the U.S. government.

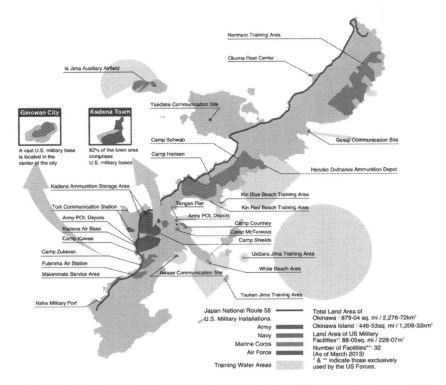

Fig. 2.1 Map of Okinawa Main Island indicating USFJ facilities. (Source: U.S. military facilities and areas on Okinawa main island and its vicinity, Okinawa Prefectural Government, Washington, DC Office)

It is also said that from the "19th century until and beyond World War II, most overseas bases throughout the world were 'automatically provided by colonial control and were an important aspect and purpose of imperial domination'" (Espiritu quoting Harkavy 2008: 28). This resonates up to this day, with the United States owning sole monopoly over the numerous military installations not only in the Asia-Pacific region but also worldwide. After the Cold War, the bases remained, and are presently considered significant in the war against terrorism and Islamic fundamentalism that the United States and its allies are waging. In the East Asian region, most of these installations are located in Japan, with three-fourths of them situated on the main island of Okinawa—a small island off the southern coast of the Japanese archipelago. With this, it is said that Okinawa is "used to project American power throughout Asia in the service of a de facto U.S. grand strategy to perpetuate or increase American hegemonic power" in Asia (Johnson 2000: 64).

The Post-War Years and the Occupation of Okinawa

With Japan's defeat in the Second World War, and to atone for its aggression and imperialist ambitions in North and South East Asia, the country had to acquiesce to American power and be occupied for seven years from 1945 to 1952. However, Okinawa was occupied for 20 more years until its reversion to Japan in 1972. From 1952 to 1972, the Government of the Ryukyu Islands (*Ryūkyū Seifu*) was created under the proclamation of the United States Civil Administration of the Ryukyus (USCAR) and was abolished in May 1972 upon Okinawa's reversion to Japan. While this government had legislative, judiciary, and executive branches, and the legislature made its own laws, the USCAR could overrule their decisions in cases of conflicts with the USCAR.

It was said that the Allied forces' attack and occupation was necessitated in order to bring the War to an end. A precursor to this was an attack on Okinawa, situated far south of the Japanese archipelago, which is within close proximity to Taiwan, China, and South East Asia. The Battle of Okinawa was said to be the longest and hardest campaigns of the Second World War and was considered to be Japan's last line of defence before it was defeated (Lie 2001: 99). Casualties in this battle were mostly civilians, and around 150,000–200,000 civilians were reported to have lost their lives. It has been largely said that Japan had sacrificed Okinawa to spare the mainland from further destruction during the War, for which the Okinawans felt betrayed.

Okinawa had always been peripheral in terms of its relations with mainland Japan. Formerly an independent kingdom, the Kingdom of the Ryukyus (Yaeyama, Miyako, Okinawa, and the Amami group of islands originally comprised the kingdom), was a group of islands with its own distinct cultural traditions, languages, and dialects. It enjoyed flourishing trade relations with its Asian neighbours in its heyday and had tributary relationships with Ming China. In 1609, the kingdom was subjugated by the Shimazu clan of the Satsuma fief in present-day Kagoshima prefecture[2] and in 1879, the Meiji government of Japan officially made the Ryukyu Islands into a prefecture, now known as Okinawa.[3] Between 1879 and

1895, the Japanese government initially sought to maintain the old Ryukyuan traditions and customs, through the "preservation of old customs policy" (Hanazaki 1996: 121) and this period was known to be the *kyūkan onzon jidai* or the period when these Ryukyuan customs were preserved (Taira 1997: 155–156). However, the government gradually changed its policies and enacted policies of "forced" cultural assimilation towards the Okinawans, wherein Okinawan customs as well as the use of the Okinawan language were prohibited. An example of this were the so-called dialect cards or the *hōgen fuda* that the students who spoke Okinawan in school were made to wear around their necks. These policies were enacted to make the Okinawans "become Japanese" (*Nihonjin ni naru*) (Tomiyama 1990). In relation to this, Tomiyama Ichiro talks about how the Okinawans were made to be "Okinawans", in the process of becoming "Japanese". Being "Okinawan" and being "Japanese" according to Tomiyama, was not in any way related to belonging to either an Okinawan or a Japanese (that is, mainland Japanese) culture. Rather, "Okinawan" can be said to be a category bestowed upon by modern Japanese society. Hence, to become "Japanese" entailed a process of modernization that called for the eradication (*fusshoku*) of qualities deemed as primitive, and thus changed into those seen as "modern", such as being hygienic from non-hygienic (*eisei/fueisei*), rational from insane (*risei/kyōki*), diligent from lazy (*kinben/taida*), and modern from primitive (*kindai/mikai*) (Tomiyama 1990: 3–5).

The perceived cultural differences (such as the Okinawan language or dialect, and the significant use and consumption of pork in the Okinawan diet) of Okinawans from the mainland Japanese may be said to have spurred discriminatory feelings towards the Okinawans, and they are considered to be "lower class Japanese". This discrimination against Okinawans was also reproduced in places where Okinawans and mainland Japanese migrated to and settled in the early years of the twentieth century, such as the Philippines and Brazil (Mori, 2003: 49–52; Ohno 2006: 92–94; Matsumura 2015: 183), as well as in Taiwan, where Okinawans were discriminated against by both Taiwanese and mainland Japanese (Matsuda 2018). Eminent historian of Okinawa, George H. Kerr, has this to say:

> An outstanding example of differentiation was the Okinawan use of pork as a main article of diet. This was part of the Chinese cultural heritage; many Okinawans established themselves in the metropolitan centers of Japan (and in Hawaii) as proprietors of piggeries. This, in Japanese eyes, placed them

almost on a level with the despised Eta, the butchers and the tanners and shoemakers of the old days. Hand-tattooing among the older women (no longer practiced) was another Okinawan irritant to Japanese sensibilities. The strong insularity of Japanese nationalism would not admit the Okinawans easily to full membership in Japanese society. (Kerr 2000: 448–449)

During the Second World War, Okinawans were recruited to serve in the Japanese Imperial Army. There were also cases wherein schoolgirls were forced to act as nurses, and this event is immortalized at the Himeyuri Monument dedicated to these girls at Itoman, a city located in the southern part of the main island. There were more civilian casualties than those of the military in this so-called Typhoon of Steel, making the Battle of Okinawa one of the bloodiest campaigns of the Second World War. Indeed, the War left Okinawa a devastated place and the Allied Occupation of the prefecture did not exactly alleviate Okinawan lives. The United States occupied Japan to ascertain that the latter would not assert its ambitious imperial policies on the region. Moreover, the former saw in the latter an ally in the Cold War against communism, hence the occupation of Okinawa which lasted until 1972 (Sarantakes 2000: xvi–xix).[4] In fact, General Douglas MacArthur, Supreme Commander of the U.S. Occupation Forces on Okinawa, on 1 September 1947, was said to have expressed opposition to a proposal by the State Department to return Okinawa to Japan at the end of the Occupation (Hein and Selden 2003: 19). In that same month, the Showa Emperor (Emperor Hirohito) was said to have sent a secret message to MacArthur requesting that the United States maintain control of Okinawa as a protection from the Soviet Union (Ibid). In the letter it was suggested that Okinawa be "leased to the U.S. on a 'twenty-five or fifty year, or even longer' basis, to facilitate U.S. opposition to communism" (McCormack 2007: 156). Also during this year, a "foreign observer" who met up with MacArthur, was said to have stated that the policy of the United States during this time was to "tie Japan politically and economically to the United States, and thus to bring the western strategic frontier of the United States face to face with Russia along the latter's boundaries on the Pacific Ocean" (Yoshida 2001: 25). This involved the "maintenance and improvement of the U.S. bases of Guam, Saipan, Iwo Jima, and Okinawa" (Ibid). Moreover, the United States would retain Okinawa even after the Occupation of Japan and "use the island as a military base with the dual mission of defending Japan and protecting other nations from the

Japanese" (Sarantakes 2000: 41). It was under the pretext of the U.S.-Japan Security Treaty that Okinawa has been burdened with the military installations of the United States for the defence and protection not only of the Asia-Pacific region but of Japan as well. However, there was no indication in the treaty that the majority of the bases should be located in Okinawa prefecture (Nomura 2005: 26).

The defining moment came on 8 September 1951 when the United States and 47 other countries signed the San Francisco Peace Treaty, where it was stipulated that Japan has full sovereignty over its territories and water, thus recognizing an end to U.S. rule in the country. However, it allowed the United States to retain control of Okinawa, as stated in Article 3 of the Treaty:

> Japan will concur in any proposal of the United States to the United Nations to place under its trusteeship, with the United States sole administering authority, Nansei Shoto south of 29 degrees north latitude (including the Ryukyu Islands and the Daito Islands), Nanto Shoto south of Sofu Gan (including the Bonin Islands, Rosario Island, and the Volcano Islands) and Parece Vela and Marcus Island. Pending the making of such a proposal and affirmative action thereon, the United States will have the right to exercise all and any powers of administration, legislation, and jurisdiction over the territory and inhabitants of these islands, including their territorial waters. (Quoted in Yoshida 2001: 50–51)

In fact, prior to the Occupation in 1945, the Okinawan islands were already seen as "essential" to form "the new strategic frontier" of the United States, along with the Philippines and the Japanese mandated islands, and hence the control and maintenance of Okinawa under U.S. rule was deemed important (Yoshida 2001: 19). In conjunction with the sheer number of military installations in Okinawa occupying a strategic position in the Asia-Pacific region, was the existence of the two largest bases in the Philippines—Clark Air Base and Subic Naval Base.[5] The creation and maintenance of military installations was of course a strategy by the United States in its fight against communism especially at the height of the Cold War. In fact, as early as 1953, U.S. Vice President Nixon visited Okinawa and said that "the United States will control Okinawa so long as the communist threat exists" (Ibid: 58). This was echoed by President Dwight Eisenhower in 1954 when he mentioned maintaining "indefinitely" the U.S. bases in Okinawa (Ibid).

Both Japan and the United States saw Okinawa's significance against the threat of communism, hence the maintenance of military troops in the prefecture was deemed important. However, this set up led the United States to opt for a "separate peace" with Japan, while occupying Okinawa as a "military colony" (McCormack 2007: 156; Yoshida 2007). This set the stage for dividing the country into a "peace state", referring to the Japanese mainland, and a "war state", alluding to Okinawa as it served as a base for wars in Korea and Vietnam, and continues to be seen as such for wars in Afghanistan, and Iraq (McCormack 2007: 122–123, 157).

During the years of the United States' occupation of Japan, the former had forced its policies on the latter, including the renunciation of war as stated in the current Japanese constitution. While Japan is now a sovereign state and Okinawa a part of it upon its reversion in 1972, Okinawa seemingly remains to be "occupied", considering the sheer number of military bases in the area—around 70 per cent of which are in this prefecture that merely occupies 0.6 per cent of Japan's territory (Hook and Siddle 2003: 3). Most of these bases are concentrated in the main island of Okinawa that occupies 10.08 per cent of Okinawa's land area (Yoshida 2008). Okinawa, thus has been dubbed the "keystone of the Pacific" (Inoue 2007: 41; Yoshida 2001: 61).

While it is said that Okinawa was not "a possession, a colony, nor a trust territory" (Kerr 2000: 3) in the formal sense of the word, in reality the occupation of Okinawa took on a seemingly colonial form. With the San Francisco Peace Treaty of 1951, Okinawa was "turned under direct military administration into a U.S. military colony" (McCormack 2007: 156). In a similar vein, Koji Taira states that what the United States had in Okinawa was a "colonial dictatorship exercised through a military government" (Taira 1997: 163). Gavan McCormack adds that whereas in the mainland, the Occupation was "benign and soft", in Okinawa it was "harsh and oppressive" (McCormack 2007: 156). The main reason for colonization was more due to Okinawa's strategic location rather than to "free the Okinawans" or to "right any wrongs" (Sarantakes 2000: 66). It should also be noted that at the time of the Occupation, Okinawa was not part of Japan—the Okinawans were stateless—they were neither part of Japan nor the United States.

During the war, Okinawans were left to think about their place in Japanese society and whether they were really considered Japanese. Their difference was strongly emphasized during the Occupation when General MacArthur was said to have stated that the "Okinawans are not Japanese"

(Tomiyama 1990: 1; Nomura 2005: 28). In line with this, U.S. insistence on a separate Ryukyuan identity, such as calling the Okinawans, Ryukyuans, and referring to Okinawa as the Ryukyus, may be seen as a way by which the Americans saw the Okinawans as separate from the Japanese. During this time also, Okinawan identity as non-Japanese was reinforced as a "rationale for transferring the stewardship of the former prefecture to the United States" (Allen 2002: 7). Ironically, this stirred up opposition from Okinawans who interpreted the move as a "racist contempt" for their being an inferior people (Taira 1997: 160). Therefore, the Okinawan response was "we are Japanese", and this response was seen as a "the most convenient weapon against American racism" (Ibid: 161). However, as I will explain later, Okinawans were also divided amongst themselves on this. On the other hand, the Okinawans would claim and insist on their distinctiveness ("We are Okinawans") vis-à-vis the Japanese. Thus, it can be said that Okinawan identity is and has been characterized by ambivalence, which is traceable to the late nineteenth century, during which Okinawa was "neither of nor not of the Japanese center", prompting Okinawans to come to terms as to who they were (Allen 2002: 5).

In the early 1950s, there were also attempts by several individuals and organizations such as the Association for Okinawan Reversion to push for a reversion to Japan. However, these calls were dismissed by the United States, associating such moves with communism. Yara Chobyo, the president of the Association for Okinawan Reversion, said that the Okinawan people desire to be part again of Japan and to "live as Japanese under Japan's constitution", and not because of any anti-American feelings (Yoshida 2001: 58). Yara's efforts were in vain.

Thus, in the years leading up to the reversion, Okinawans were caught between choosing to stay under American rule, or be back in the hands of Japan, in spite of the history of subjugation that characterized Okinawa's relationship with the latter. While the Okinawans could choose to be totally independent from the Japanese mainland, there was still a clamour to be part of it, especially in the 1960s when Okinawans rallied for the prefecture's reversion to Japan. This was in part due to the atrocities committed by the American soldiers on the locals. Another was the Okinawan sentiment against U.S. aggression in Vietnam. Okinawa's strategic location and proximity to Vietnam and the number of American bases present in the prefecture highlighted Okinawa's importance as an American military outpost during the Vietnam War.

Another reason for the desire for reversion is the Okinawan's identification with the Japanese nation. They see themselves as belonging to the Japanese nation, and hence, they are Japanese. In 1967, public opinion in both Japan and Okinawa about the issue was surveyed. From the Okinawan sample, those who desired reversion gave reasons such as "we are Japanese" and "Japan is our fatherland". From the Japanese sample, on the other hand, reasons such as "Okinawa is historically part of the Japanese mainland" and "the Okinawan people are Japanese" indicated the mainland Japanese's desire for Okinawa's reversion. Majority (85 per cent) of both Japanese and Okinawan respondents gave the above as reasons (Watanabe 1970: 3). Meanwhile, on 9 August 1965, then Prime Minister Sato Eisaku, the first prime minister to visit Okinawa while in office had this to say: "Without the return of Okinawa to its homeland, the post-war period is not over for Japan" (Funabashi 1999: 133). In 1972, the Occupation period had formally ended for Okinawa, and Okinawa has regained its prefectural status with Okinawans becoming "Japanese" and enjoying the same constitutional rights as any other Japanese. Despite this, however, there were some Okinawans who voiced out their anger at the terms of the agreement of the reversion to Japan, saying that it will only be a "new annexation" of Okinawa, which would mean the continued presence of the U.S. military bases in the prefecture (Yokota 2017: 59). Kuba Masahiko, then Professor of Economics at the University of the Ryukyus was said to have stated that the reversion to Japan that Okinawans wanted was not only the transfer of administrative authority from the United States to the Japanese mainland, but the removal of the U.S. military bases on Okinawa (Ibid: 67). The sentiments that part of the Okinawan population had at the time of reversion can be said to continue up to this day, where Okinawans feel that they are being burdened with hosting most of the military bases in Japan, and thus seemingly still "occupied" by the U.S. military.

The U.S. Bases in Present-day Okinawa

It can be said that Okinawa continues to be "occupied" to this day as attested to by the vast number of U.S. bases dotting the prefecture. To say that the Occupation has ended in 1972, is an anachronism of sorts as the current conditions in Okinawa negate what was supposed to be the (formal) end of American rule in 1972.

In 1995, the Pentagon (with Tokyo acknowledging) declared that "Asia remains an area of uncertainty, tension, and immense concentration of military power" and the United States reinstated its "commitment" to maintain around 100,000 troops in the future (Inoue 2007: 4). Forty-seven years after its reversion to Japan in May 1972, Okinawa still finds itself engulfed in issues and problems linked to the American presence in the prefecture. This said, it is apparent that Okinawa found itself entangled within the web of politics and issues of security in East Asia and the U.S.-Japan Alliance. This current position of Okinawa may be sustained in the near future unless the current Trump administration works to reduce the number of U.S. bases in the southern island. An article in the 24 November 2016 issue of *The Washington Post* reported that some Okinawans have a thin glimmer of hope that Donald Trump will effect a change on Okinawa: "Lots of people are saying the same thing—that they have a tiny hope that something will change, that Donald Trump might reduce the burden of military bases on Okinawa." Moreover, the election of the first Amerasian politician, Tamaki Denny, as successor to former governor Onaga Takeshi, who succumbed to pancreatic cancer in August 2018, signals a continued struggle against the construction of a military base in Henoko, as well as the fight for the reduction of military bases on the island. Tamaki, the son of an Okinawan mother and a U.S. serviceman father who he never met, won in the gubernatorial elections held on 30 September 2018 on an anti-base platform.

The creation of U.S. military installations in the immediate post-war period necessitated the expropriation of lands owned by the locals, many of them farm lands. A lot of these people who lost their lands were relocated to other areas, but these areas were small and many of them were made to fit in these places. Such was the case in Chatan Town where the U.S. military facilities occupied areas that once were rice paddies and agricultural lands (Yoshida 2001: 60). In Yomitan Town and Ginowan City, numerous farmers were also kept off their lands to make way for the creation of the bases. Some of the people were also forced out of their lands by bulldozers and bayonets, particularly those living in Isahama on the main island of Okinawa and Ie-jima, an island off the Motobu Peninsula (Amemiya 1996; Yoshida 2001: 65). In the 1950s, around 250,000 Okinawans were forcibly evicted from their lands for this purpose (some were even forced at bayonet point), whereas others became exiles to South America, in countries such as Bolivia, Argentina, and Peru (McCormack 2007: 174). These forced evictions are testament to the blatant usurpation of rights (i.e. human rights and property rights) of the Okinawan people. McCormack adds that these forced evictions resembled those that occurred in Diego Garcia, an island in the Chagos Archipelago on the Indian Ocean, where summary evictions of residents were carried out for the construction of an American military base in the 1960s. This is in contrast to the Japanese mainland where most of the land (around 87 per cent) used for these military facilities are government-owned, while in Okinawa's case, national land accounts for only around 23 per cent, with the rest being privately owned lands, prefectural lands, and municipal lands (Military Base Division, Okinawa Prefectural Government).

Yoshida moreover states that the enactment of the Peace Treaty on 28 August 1952, was also the time when Japan "abandoned" Okinawa to a foreign power. During this time, the Okinawans also "lost their legal basis to press the United States for compensation for the use of their land prior to 28 April 1952, as a result of the treaty terms by which Japan waived all war claims of its nationals against the United States" (Yoshida 2001: 52).

Moreover, one should not overlook the fact that Japan pays for the existence of the bases, and for the Japanese civilian employees' (who are employed as government employees) salaries and wages, including bonuses. As Chalmers Johnson says, the United States has military bases in 19 countries, but it is only in Japan that the host government pays for all the costs of local employees (Johnson 2000: 55). It is also said that Japan allots around five billion U.S. dollars a year for the bases that are in the country (Cumings 2009: 402). It was said that a secret agreement regarding the payment of the bases had existed between the United States and Japan. In 1971, the *Mainichi Shimbun* was said to have disclosed an agreement between the two countries that Japan would shoulder the 4,000,000 dollars (U.S.) needed for the restoration of the U.S.-held land to its "original state" (Yoshida 2001: 159). Meanwhile, in 1998, University of the Ryukyus Professor Gabe Masaaki was said to have discovered a document saying that the Japanese government had not only secretly agreed to the five-billion-dollar payment but also to an additional 160,000,000 dollars for the improvement and relocation of the military facilities (Ibid). Apparently, the Japanese government denied this. It can be argued here that the Japanese government is complicit with the government of the United States in perpetuating American military presence in Okinawa, thus sustaining the ongoing "occupation" of the prefecture. While primarily political, this needs to be seen as not only an issue of politics, but as something that had cultural and social repercussions on the lives of ordinary people during the 27-year Occupation period and continues to do so in contemporary times.

Nevertheless, despite the highly political nature of the base issue and the continued American military presence in Japan, which is concentrated in Okinawa, a large number of Okinawans are against the presence of the U.S. bases in the prefecture, since aside from the various problems associated with the presence of the U.S. military and these installations, not a few Okinawans feel that they are indirectly responsible for the U.S. wars in Iraq and Afghanistan by leasing their land to the U.S. bases:

> The islanders' strong resistance against hosting U.S. military bases is inseparable from their experience of the indescribable horrors of a war that took more than one fourth of the lives of local people. They do not just want to see another war in Okinawa; many feel responsible for indirectly participating in current U.S. wars in Iraq and Afghanistan, by providing land for their military bases, however reluctantly. (Norimatsu 2010: 2)

However, it should be noted that there are people who somehow agree to the continued existence of the bases, as it also translates into livelihood for them. These people belong to the working class as well as small businesspeople (most of them own small shops, bars, etc. in the vicinity of the bases), who rely on the presence of the U.S. military for their income. Not to mention the private landowners that earn lease payments from these installations built on their properties. Among this group of people who hope for the continued existence of the bases, at least in their lifetime, include people working inside these military installations; those who favour the existence of the U.S. bases mainly for economic reasons and job security. These people are locals (both mainland Japanese and Okinawan), migrant workers, and people of Japanese and Okinawan descent.

In the next chapter, I situate the Occupation of Okinawa in a transnational context by looking at transnational movements of people, goods, information, and so on not only between the United States and Japan/Okinawa, but in a more regional (i.e. Asia-Pacific) context. I argue that the Occupation of Okinawa should also be regarded as a transnational project that involved actors other than the U.S. and the Japanese governments; among them, people who worked on the construction of these military installations as well as for the maintenance and the functioning of these bases.

NOTES

1. Up until 2016, Okinawa hosted around 75 per cent (74.5 per cent) of the U.S. military bases in Japan (See Defense of Japan pamphlet, 2016, page 255). However, with the return of 4000 hectares of the Northern Training Area in 2016, along with other areas, the total acreage used for U.S. military facilities in Okinawa was reduced to around 70 per cent at present. (See Defense of Japan pamphlet 2018, page 17, and the Okinawa Times article, "Okinawa Prepares for New Effort to Block Henoko Base", 13 January 2017.)
2. During the Tokugawa era (despite having a tributary relationship with Tokugawa Japan), the kingdom still maintained its tributary status with China. Its relationship with Japan, however, was hidden from the Qing court.
3. The Amami Islands however became part of Kagoshima prefecture.
4. One should not overlook as well the fact that Okinawa was used by Japanese officials to achieve independence for the mainland in 1952, with Okinawa being left under U.S. military control.
5. Due to a 12-11 Senate decision to reject a new military treaty between the United States and the Philippines, both the Clark and Subic bases were ejected from the country in 16 September 1992 (Brillantes 1992: 141).

REFERENCES

(2017, January 13). Okinawa Prepares for New Effort to Block Henoko Base by Rallying Local Opposition. *Okinawa Times*, https://www.okinawatimes.co.jp/articles/-/79730. Accessed 25 May 2019. (2019, February 25).

Abe Moves Ahead with Base Work in Okinawa after 'No' Referendum. *The Asahi Shimbun*. http://www.asahi.com/ajw/articles/AJ201902250039.html. Accessed 6 Mar 2019.

Allen, M. (2002). *Identity and Resistance in Okinawa*. Lanham: Rowman & Littlefield Publishers, Inc.

Amemiya, K. (1996, October 25). *The Bolivian Connection: U.S. Bases and Okinawan Emigration* (Japan Policy Research Institute Working Paper no. 25). http://www.jpri.org/publications/workingpapers/wp25.html. Accessed 10 Oct 2018.

Brillantes, A. B. J. (1992, February). The Philippines in 1991: Disasters and Decisions. *Asian Survey (A Survey of Asia in 1991: Part II), 32*(2), 140–145.

Cumings, B. (2009). *Dominion from Sea to Sea: Pacific Ascendancy and American Power*. New Haven: Yale University Press.

Defense of Japan Pamphlet 2016 Section 4: Stationing of the U.S. Forces in Japan. Ministry of Defence, Japan. https://www.mod.go.jp/e/publ/w_paper/pdf/2016/DOJ2016_2-4-4_web.pdf. Accessed 25 May 2019.

Defense of Japan Pamphlet 2018. Ministry of Defence, Japan. https://www.mod.go.jp/e/publ/w_paper/pdf/2018/DOJ2018_Full_1130.pdf. Accessed 25 May 2019.

Espiritu, Y. L. (2008). *Homebound: Filipino American Lives Across Cultures, Communities, and Countries* (Philippine ed.). Quezon City: Ateneo de Manila University Press.

Fifield, A. (2016, November 24). For military-weary Okinawa, Donald Trump offers a glimmer of hope. *The Washington Post*. https://www.washingtonpost.com/world/asia_pacific/for-military-weary-okinawa-donald-trump-offers-a-glimmer-of-hope/2016/11/24/da8140eb-0939-4a03-ae9d-0855795ff32d_story.html?utm_term=.d774fc0d81e9. Accessed 10 Oct 2018.

Funabashi, Y. (1999). *Alliance Adrift*. New York: Council on Foreign Relations, Inc.

Hanazaki, K. (1996). Ainu Moshir and Yaponesia: Ainu and Okinawan Identities in Contemporary Japan. In D. Denoon, M. Hudson, G. McCormack, & T. Morris-Suzuki (Eds.), *Multicultural Japan: Palaeolithic to Postmodern* (pp. 117–132). Cambridge: Cambridge University Press.

Hook, G. D., & Siddle, R. (Eds.). (2003). *Japan and Okinawa: Structure and Subjectivity*. London: Routledge.

Hein, L., & Selden, M. (2003). Culture, Power, and Identity in Contemporary Okinawa. In L. Hein & M. Selden (Eds.), *Islands of Discontent: Okinawan Responses to Japanese and American Power* (pp. 1–36). Lanham: Rowman and Littlefield Publishers, Inc.

Iacobelli, P. (2017). James Tigner and the Okinawan Emigration Program to Latin America. In J. Moreno & B. Tatar (Eds.), *Transnational Frontiers of Asia and Latin America Since 1800* (pp. 255–266). London: Routledge.

Iacobelli, P. (2018). Okinawa and the Fear of World War Three. In T. Morris-Suzuki (Ed.), *The Korean War in Asia: A Hidden History* (pp. 109–128). Lanham: Rowman & Littlefield.

Inoue, M. S. (2007). *Okinawa and the U.S. Military: Identity Making in the Age of Globalization*. New York: Columbia University Press.

Johnson, C. (2000). *Blowback: The Costs and Consequences of American Empire*. New York: Henry Holt and Company, LLC.

Johnson, C. (2004). *The Sorrows of Empire: Militarism, Secrecy, and the End of the Republic*. London: Verso.

Kerr, G. H. (2000). *Okinawa: The History of an Island People* (Revised ed.). Boston: Tuttle Publishing.

Lie, J. (2001). *Multi-Ethnic Japan*. Cambridge: Harvard University Press.

Lutz, C. (2009). *The Bases of Empire: The Global Struggle against U.S. Military Posts*. New York: New York University Press.

Matsuda, H. (2018). *Liminality of the Japanese Empire: Border Crossings from Okinawa to Colonial Taiwan*. Honolulu: University of Hawaii Press.

Matsumura, W. (2015). *The Limits of Okinawa: Japanese Capitalism, Living Labor, and Theorizations of Community*. Durham: Duke University Press.
McCormack, G. (2007). *Client State: Japan in the American Embrace*. London: Verso.
Military Base Division. Okinawa Prefectural Government. http://dc-office.org/basedata. Accessed 29 May 2019.
Mori, K. (2003). Identity Formations among Okinawans and Their Descendants in Brazil. In J. Lesser (Ed.), *Searching for Home Abroad: Japanese Brazilians and Transnationalism* (pp. 47–65). Durham: Duke University Press.
Nomura, K. (2005). *Muishiki no Shokuminchishugi: Nihonjin no Beigunkichi to Okinawajin*. Tokyo: Ochanomizu Shobō.
Norimatsu, S. (2010, September 20). The World is beginning to know Okinawa: Ota Masahide Reflects on his Life from the Battle of Okinawa to the Struggle for Okinawa. *The Asia-Pacific Journal, 38*(4–10), 1–16.
Ohno, S. (2006). The Intermarried Issei and Mestizo Nisei in the Philippines: Reflections on the Origin of Philippine Nikkeijin Problems. In N. Adachi (Ed.), *Japanese Diasporas: Unsung Pasts, Conflicting Presents, and Uncertain Futures* (pp. 85–101). London: Routledge.
Sarantakes, N. E. (2000). *Keystone: The American Occupation of Okinawa and U.S.-Japanese Relations*. College Station: Texas A&M University Press.
Taira, K. (1997). Troubled National Identity: The Ryukyuans/Okinawans. In M. Weiner (Ed.), *Japan's Minorities: The Illusion of Homogeneity* (pp. 140–177). London: Routledge.
Tomiyama, I. (1990). *Kindai Nihon Shakai to "Okinawajin": Nihonjin ni naru to iu koto*. Tokyo: Nihon Keizai Hyōronsha.
Watanabe, A. (1970). *The Okinawa Problem: A Chapter in Japan-U.S. Relations*. Victoria: Melbourne University Press.
Yokota, R. (2017). Reversion-Era Proposals for Okinawan Regional Autonomy. In P. Iacobelli & H. Matsuda (Eds.), *Rethinking Postwar Okinawa: Beyond American Occupation* (pp. 59–79). Lanham: Lexington Books.
Yoshida, K. (2001). *Democracy Betrayed: Okinawa Under U.S. Occupation*. Bellingham: Centre for East Asian Studies, Western Washington University.
Yoshida, K. (2007). *"Gunji Shokuminchi" Okinawa: Nihon Hondo to no "Ondosa" no Shōtai*. Tokyo: Kōbunken.
Yoshida, K. (2008, August 1). US Bases, Japan, and the Reality of Okinawa as a Military Colony. *The Asia-Pacific Journal, 6*(8), 1–11.

CHAPTER 3

Transnational Movements During the Occupation of Okinawa: Third Country Nationals and the U.S. Bases

> *The United States Army now foresees a need for about 8000 Filipino labourers to be employed directly by the United States outside the Philippines including the Mariananas-Bonins [sic], Okinawa and elsewhere in the Pacific.*
> Nathaniel P. Davis, Charge d'Affaires ad interim, 13 May 1947
> (Recruitment of Filipino Laborers and Employees by the United States Army, Treaties and International Acts Series 3646, p. 1.)

On 13 and 16 of May 1947, an agreement regarding the recruitment of Filipino labourers and employees by the U.S. Army was signed in Manila. This agreement was effected by an "exchange of notes" between the American Charge d'Affaires ad interim Nathaniel Davis and the Philippine Acting Secretary of Foreign Affairs Bernabe Africa, and it entered into force on 16 May 1947. To the request quoted above, Africa replied on 16 May 1947 that the "Philippine Government approves the plan and conditions" and that "authority is hereby granted to the United States Army to recruit Filipino laborers and employees and to ship them to the desired areas without documentation and prior consultation with the Philippine government" (Recruitment of Filipino Laborers and Employees by the United States Army, Treaties and International Acts Series 3646: 4). Africa requested that a list of these Filipino labourers and employees, containing their full names, date, and place of birth, as well as addresses in the Philippines, be submitted to the Department of Foreign Affairs in the Philippines.

Meanwhile, on 21 September 1947, Carlos Amoranto, a native of Los Baños, Laguna, arrived in Okinawa. He was among the Filipinos recruited to work on U.S. military bases stationed on the island at that time. He was recruited by the U.S. Army to work for the Choirmaster Laundry as a clerk typist, to which he told them: "you are sending me to Okinawa as a clerk typist and I don't [even] know what a typewriter is?" He, along with other Filipino workers, was sent to Okinawa on board a "big ship". When they arrived, Carlos said that he was rather assigned to be timekeeper at the laundry. Carlos was not a stranger working for the Americans as he experienced working with the U.S. Army Engineering Corps based in the Philippines when he was 17.

Eight years after, an electrical engineering student named Enrico Jamora, was recruited by the U.S. Army Special Services in 1955 to play in Japan as a member of a brass band. Enrico started his music career in the Philippines as a staff musician in a local TV programme, called CBN Canteen, while saving up for his education. Things changed though upon arrival in Okinawa, where he stayed on to work as a musician playing for U.S. bases in the region, including those in Korea.

These two Filipinos, who I will be talking more about later, were among the thousands recruited to work on U.S. military bases in Okinawa during the American Occupation. These labourers and employees are collectively known as "Third Country Nationals" or "TCNs" employed by the U.S. military to assist in the operation of its military installations all over the globe. This highlights a significant migration stream from the Philippines to Okinawa during the immediate post-war period, and the United States' crucial role in this particular migration process. Moreover, the employment of TCNs has illustrated (and continues to do so) the inherent hierarchies in base employment that is not only reflective of a segmented labour force that entails differences in pay scale, but also points to hierarchies in national identification and/or belonging as well as stratification according to social class and gender. As Cynthia Enloe states, bases should also be seen as "artificial societies created out of unequal relations between men and women of different races and classes" (Enloe 2000: 2).

This chapter situates the Occupation of Okinawa in a transnational context by looking at transnational movements of people, goods, information, and services in a more regional—that is, Asia-Pacific—context, rather than solely between the United States and Japan. I argue that the

Occupation of Okinawa should be regarded as a transnational project that involved actors other than the U.S. and Japanese governments. For this chapter, focus is given on what could be considered to be the least looked-at actor in military basing—civilian base workers. Moreover, this also reflects how Okinawa became a "contact zone" (Pratt 1992) for those situated at the lowest ranks of the U.S. military, as well as "racial minorities and colonial subjects" (Shimabuku 2019: 50).

TCNs and the Global Hierarchy of Base Work

In any base construction, there is always a demand for contractors and labour power; and in the case of American military base constructions, TCNs or Third Country Nationals make up a significant number of the labour force, as well as employees who staff these military installations for purposes they purportedly serve. A large number of this labour source are usually former colonials, such as Filipinos, who take on the bulk of these jobs. This is true when bases were built (and continue to be built) in the Asia-Pacific, where Filipinos and other nationals were hired to assist in the building of these military installations in Okinawa, as well as in Vietnam and Thailand, where Filipino and Korean labour were brought in for this purpose, as well as to add to the current labour force comprising "local nationals" or LNs. In recent years, the hiring of TCNs still continues for work on these military installations. Due in part to close relations between the United States and the Philippines, which can be traced to the former's 50-year colonization of the archipelago, Filipinos have become a preferred workforce for the reason that they speak and understand English and are familiar with American customs.

At present, TCNs are also employed in bases in Iraq and Afghanistan, where nationals of the Global South (that is, South and South East Asia) work alongside LNs (Eichler 2014: 601). Filipinos also make up a significant percentage of the workforce in U.S. military installations in Iraq. At the outset, base construction is a boon to nationals of much less economically developed countries as it translates into work for these people. While the economic gains that have been made accessible to these TCNs cannot be discounted, these military bases are testament to the ongoing and growing gap between the United States and the countries in the periphery, as well as an undeniable "sense of racial, cultural, or social superiority" (Lutz 2009: 7) emanating from the imperial centre.

TCNs, according to the U.S. Department of State are persons who are *neither citizens of the United States nor of the host country where they are assigned* (italics, mine). Likewise, permanent legal resident aliens of the United States are not considered TCNs (USAID Foreign Service National Personnel Administration, ADS Chapter 495: 13). Moreover, TCNs are defined as persons who meet the following criteria (as stated in the U.S. Department of State Unclassified Document on TCNs: 1):

1. If employed, is eligible for return travel to the TCN's home country or country from which recruited at U.S. Government expense.
2. Is on a limited appointment for a specific period of time.
3. Encumbers a direct-hire, personal service agreement (PSA) or personal service contract (PSC) FSN[1] position covered under the local compensation plan. Such an employee normally is recruited from outside the host country and relocated from the point of recruitment to the host country. The return travel obligation assumed by the U.S. Government may have been the obligation of another employer in the area of assignment if the employee has been in substantially continuous employment which provided for the TCN's return to home country or country from which recruited.
4. For USAID, TCNs employed under a PSC are subject to provisions of AID HB 14 (AIDAR).

The United States Agency for International Development (USAID) document also states that TCNs are required to go home to their country of recruitment within 30 days "after the termination or completion of the contract or forfeit all rights to the repatriation" (USAID, ADS Chapter 495: 13). TCNs are essentially temporary workforce bound by contracts.

The hiring of TCNs become necessary when there are no qualified persons in the host country to take on some specific jobs. TCNs are also hired when the training of persons in the host country (i.e. LNs) is difficult due to time and other constraints. In the U.S. Department of State Unclassified Document on TCNs, it is also stated that the hiring of TCNs will be effected if "program efficiency and policy objectives can be achieved only by using TCNs as a temporary substitute for available, eligible and qualified U.S. citizens and persons from the host country" (U.S. Department of State Unclassified Document on TCNs: 2). This calls to mind the immediate post-war conditions in Okinawa that necessitated the hiring of TCNs amid the available human resources in the host society. Several can be mentioned here: (1) the lack of able-bodied personnel to help in base construction as well as staffing of these military installations; (2) a language barrier between the occupying forces and the locals; and (3) the "former enemy" status of the Japanese (and Okinawans) that can be seen to be related to issues of "trust".

The hiring of foreign workers is commonly done to address imbalance in the supply of, and demand for labour, especially when there is a surplus of jobs available. It is also common knowledge that hiring workers to do menial work or less-skilled labour attracts people who are willing to work on lower wages, and these people usually come from lower-income countries or those countries located in the periphery of the current world system. This is also the case with regards to TCNs recruited to work in base construction and service sectors on base. TCNs are (and were) hired as a cheaper labour force that were willing to work on lower wages (Barker 2009: 232). Lower skilled work which pays less than other kinds of employment on base becomes attractive to these men, who will have to content themselves with much lower wages in their home countries. These TCNs also work alongside LNs, who themselves are paid lower wages, and in the case of Okinawa during the Occupation Period, were even paid at much lower levels. This was also seen in the case of Carlos, mentioned at the beginning of this chapter, who had experienced working for the U.S. Army Engineering Corps in the Philippines. He was tasked to work in the kitchen, along with two other Filipinos who he supervised. Carlos's case, as well as that of the other two Filipinos', illustrates how LNs and TCNs then and now are being hired to work on jobs that the U.S. military and other U.S. citizens working on base would not take on. This is also due to the fact that TCNs—mostly coming from lower-income countries—are willing to take on these kinds of jobs for less pay, thus reinforcing the income hierarchy that exists. While income levels vary across skills, it cannot be denied that the stratification according to skill levels also suggests inequalities not only among nationalities, but also along racial lines. It should be noted that Carlos also lacked certain skills and cultural capital needed to qualify him for a better position, as he only was able to attend school up to the elementary level due to his family's impoverished condition. Enrico also echoed this, when he told me that during the immediate post-war years, the music industry on base was mostly composed of Filipino nationals. He added that Americans were not part of the playing bands since they would have to be paid higher rates, which most clubs would not be able to afford. This indicates the reason why Filipinos dominated the music scene at that time—they were willing to take on work regardless of the (low) rates of pay.

Maya Eichler (2014), in her work on citizenship and the recruitment of TCNs to work on U.S. military installations, said that hiring workers outside the U.S. citizenry as well as the reliance on the "global inequalities of citizenship", "simultaneously intersect" with gendered, racialized, and classed inequalities (Eichler 2014: 600). This is reflective of the immediate post-war years in Okinawa, where a pay-scale hierarchy putting U.S. citizens on top and Okinawans at the bottom speaks of various inequalities that were present within and among various groups of peoples in this particular space of the U.S. military base. This is also echoed by Carlos when he told me how he would encounter Okinawan workers—originally farmers—who were using someone else's name in order to earn a living. With the severe social and economic conditions the Okinawans experienced during the War's aftermath, it is no surprise that the locals would go as far as to use someone else's name in order to find a means of livelihood.

The Entry of TCNs in Occupied Okinawa

The American Occupation of Japan from 1945 to 1952, which lasted until 1972 in Okinawa, entailed the construction of military installations in the whole country. This led to a so-called construction boom (Sellek 2003: 82) that saw a demand for people to work on the building of these facilities, as well as those who will comprise the labour force necessary for the functioning of these military installations, such as service workers and professionals. Apart from American civilian employees, TCNs were hired to work on these military bases in Okinawa and mainland Japan. Majority of these TCNs were Filipinos who occupied mostly white-collar occupations, with some even serving in the USCAR or the United States Civil Administration of the Ryukyus in Okinawa (Tobaru 1998: 31). A large number of these Filipino TCNs landed in contractual work as labourers, cooks, and clerks, while the professional workforce comprised of engineers, medical doctors, musicians, and other white-collar workers (Yu-Jose 2002: 117). Mainland Japanese were also hired and worked as TCNs in Okinawa (Ibid: 110). While majority of the TCNs were male, there were also a few women hired to work on base. Many of these Filipino women occupied stereotypically female occupations such as domestic workers and laundrywomen (Ohno 1991: 243; Suzuki and Tamaki 1996: 70). Albeit scant, there were also professional women who worked on base during the Occupation Period.[2]

The recruitment, employment, and the migration to Okinawa of these Filipino TCNs occurred during the early years of the Occupation. The period between 1945 and 1960—the first 15 years of the Occupation—is, in particular, significant as it was also during this period (particularly in the late 1950s) that the number of TCNs was significantly reduced; in 1958, their numbers decreased to only 4.2 per cent of the total civilian work force, which excludes American nationals (Yu-Jose 2002: 112). Thus, it can be surmised that this 15-year period spans the start of the TCNs' work in Okinawa up until the termination of their contracts.

Recruitment for labour was carried out in Manila, which saw numerous Filipino men applying for these jobs on base, with some even coming from provinces not exactly in close proximity to the Philippine capital. These jobs ranged from the semi-skilled to professional white-collar occupations, such as doctors, lawyers, and engineers. It was said that the Americans preferred people who could speak English, and Filipinos were given preference as they were also educated in an American educational system (Ohno 1991: 242). This, of course, also points to the Philippines' status as an erstwhile American colony. One Nisei whom I spoke with in 2010, Sonny Uechi, shared that recruitment during this period included exams. Meanwhile, Marco Yara, whom I introduced at the beginning of this book, mentioned that there was hearsay among the elderly in Okinawa that the Americans would call out to people on the streets of Manila at that time and whoever was interested and fit for the job were hired. With this, it would seem that there was no formal recruitment policy nor criteria for Filipino labour on base. However, it is a known fact that the recruitment and outsourcing of labour from other countries is a complex web that entails various actors and processes; and in this case, state-level relations definitely come into play. At the beginning of this chapter, I gave excerpts of correspondence between the American Charge d'Affaires and the Philippine Acting Secretary of Foreign Affairs to illustrate this.

Meanwhile, base employees are categorized into four: (Nagumo 1996: 33)

1. Workers who receive their salaries from the U.S. defence budget
2. Workers who receive their salaries from U.S. government agencies' disbursements based on an independent profit system
3. House maids
4. Workers of agencies or companies carrying out their business inside the bases, such as construction companies

In an interview with a former Filipino base worker, Ohno (1991: 243) states that there are three types of Filipino workers who went to Okinawa: (1) those who went as soldiers (i.e. Philippine Scouts); (2) those who worked as employees for the military and the American government in Okinawa; and (3) those who were contracted to work in construction-related jobs, as drivers, engineers, and so on. The Philippine Scouts were known to be the first group of Filipinos who went to Occupied Okinawa. These soldiers formed part of the American forces stationed at Okinawa, replacing the first Amphibious Truck Company, which was composed of African-Americans (Yu-Jose 2002: 117). The African-American soldiers who formed part of this group were re-deployed to Osaka due to complaints against them, which included misbehaviour and trespassing into civilian areas, to more serious crimes such as rape (Ibid). The Philippine Scouts, however, were not any better than these African-Americans they replaced. It was said that these Filipinos committed grave acts against the locals as "revenge" for the atrocities perpetrated by Japanese soldiers in the Philippines during the Second World War. Due to these misdemeanours, the Philippine Scouts were repatriated to the Philippines, having spent only around two years and four months in Okinawa (Tobaru 1998: 31; Yu-Jose 2002: 110). There were reports that these Scouts were even more "dangerous" than the African-American soldiers (Shimabuku 2019: 50).

Thousands of Filipino workers, such as Carlos and Enrico who were mentioned at the beginning of this chapter, were also hired to work in Okinawa during this period. They were the second and third types of workers mentioned above. Large numbers of Filipinos went to Okinawa to work on base from the late 1940s to the early 1950s (Ohno 1991: 243). Most of these Filipino workers occupied high positions due in part to their English proficiency resulting from the establishment of an American-style mass education in the archipelago. However, the Okinawans had to content themselves with manual labour (*nikutai rōdō*) (Ohno 1991: 233). The Filipinos were paid in dollars in accordance with the 1947 Agreement between the United States and the Philippines (Treaties and Other International Act Series 3646), which states that "Filipino workers on Okinawa will receive wages based on the dollar cost rates being paid for similar work in the Philippines, plus a 25 percent overseas differential".[3] The Filipinos occupied a high position in the pay scale, next only to Americans, with the mainland Japanese ranking third, and the Okinawans fourth and at the bottom of the pay scale (Amemiya 1996; Yoshida 2001: 30; Sellek 2003: 82; Yoshida 2007: 82).

Table 3.1 illustrates the lowest and the highest hourly wages in U.S. dollars received by these four groups.

According to Yoshida, the workers were paid in B-yen currency with Okinawans receiving the lowest hourly wage (Yoshida 2007: 82). Yoshida enumerated the hourly wages of the workers in B-yen, which I arranged into a table (Table 3.2) below.

Looking at Table 3.1 below, the gaps in the wage levels of these four groups are startlingly apparent with an almost 42 per cent gap between Filipino workers who received the highest wage at 3.77 U.S. dollars per hour, to those of U.S. citizens who received 6.52 dollars per hour. This increased two-fold to around 84 per cent between U.S. citizens and Japanese and to around 94 per cent between Americans and Okinawans. Filipinos, despite occupying a high position in the pay-scale hierarchy, were said to be paid "local wage rates" even during the early years of the Occupation, as per a document from the PHILRYCOM (Philippines-Ryukyus Command) to the General Headquarters of the Far East Command on 8 January 1947:

> Policy of this command has been to employ Filipino Nationals under local wage rates. Only US continental citizens are employed at US rates of pay. Those US citizens of Filipino extraction who were born in US, and any Filipinos who were US Civil Service employees within continental US prior

Table 3.1 Base workers' wages in U.S. dollars

Nationality	Lowest wage paid per hour	Highest wage paid per hour
American	1.20	6.52
Filipino	52 cents	3.77
Japanese	83 cents	1.03
Okinawan	10 cents	36 cents

Source: Kokusekibetsu no Chingin Taikei, in Nagumo, *Beigun Kichi to Rōdō Undō*, p. 39

Table 3.2 Base Workers' Wages in B-yen

Nationality	Lowest wage paid per hour	Highest wage paid per hour
American	125.2	751.2
Filipino	48	196.8
Japanese	25	45
Okinawan	9.5	25

to being assigned this command are only Filipinos receiving US rates of pay. This Hq does not concur in employment of Filipinos at US rates unless they meet requirements indicated above.[4]

As gleaned from the above document, only Filipinos who have acquired U.S. citizenship or were U.S.-born, and those who were employed in the U.S. civil service were eligible to be paid at U.S. rates. In short, only those who have U.S. citizenship are able to access U.S. wage rates and those who are not citizens are excluded from this, despite working for the U.S. Occupation Forces and being under U.S. jurisdiction during this period. This case illustrates a seeming "global inequality of citizenship" (Eichler 2014) that had been present even during the time when the United States was just starting to establish its military might in the Asia-Pacific region through the military bases it began constructing with contracted labour from outside of its citizenry, mostly by former colonials (i.e. Filipinos) and the locals hosting these military installations (i.e. Okinawans). Needless to say, the defeated enemy—the mainland Japanese—were also hired as TCNs albeit receiving much lower pay than the Filipinos.

Meanwhile, by the late 1940s to the early 1950s, there were an estimated 6000 Filipinos in Okinawa, 90 per cent of which were male, with around half of them single (Ohno 1991: 243; Tobaru 1998: 31). A large number of these Filipinos co-habited or married Okinawan women. It was due to their relatively higher salaries among base workers that made them more attractive as marriage partners (Suzuki and Tamaki 1996: 88). When the work contracts of these Filipinos expired, most of them went back to the Philippines, bringing their wives and children with them. There were claims that some of these contracts were unjustly terminated, which I explore later in this chapter.

There were also cases wherein only the Filipino husband went back to his country, leaving his Okinawan wife and child(ren) behind (Ohno 1991: 243). Meanwhile, cases wherein the Filipino husband never returned to the Philippines are not few (Suzuki and Tamaki 1996: 71–70). Some of them still work on base (despite their advanced age) and some of them have had their nationalities changed from Philippine to American, whereas others maintained their Philippine nationality and are permanent residents. Several of these former TCNs became naturalized Japanese when they decided to make Okinawa their home. Among these are Carlos and Enrico, who I met and spoke with in late 2012 and early 2013 during one of my visits to Okinawa. Both of them married Okinawan women, acquired Japanese nationality, and continue to live their lives in Okinawa.

Being the "Other" Occupier: Situating the TCN

While it cannot be denied that the motivating factor for TCNs to work on base is largely economic, and that for many of them, working on U.S. military installations will give them more financial stability than remaining in their home countries, macro-level factors such as global economic inequities during this time should also be taken into consideration. Moreover, as I mentioned earlier, TCNs are recruited only if there is a need for a temporary substitute for available and qualified persons, who are either U.S. citizens or those from the host country.

In the case of Okinawa, the language barrier as well as the lack of qualified people could have been impediments in hiring LNs, thus the need to take in TCNs from countries such as the Philippines. This becomes a significant aspect from the perspective of U.S.-Japan relations as well as in problematizing the Occupation of Okinawa, because of the presence of other actors such as TCNs in the whole scheme of things.

The issue of class nevertheless plays a role in the recruitment and employment of TCNs for work on base. Much like entering the military, working as a TCN was a way for many of these people to augment their family's income, and for some, a way to get out of poverty. In Carlos' case, growing up impoverished in a town outside of Manila made him seek work at the young age of 17 with the U.S. Army Engineering Corps. He also mentioned that he was drafted into the Philippine Army during the Second World War. Even before the Philippine government started sending out labour migrants as a policy in the 1970s in order to address the country's economic woes, several Filipinos saw work abroad as a panacea to the economic and financial difficulties experienced in the Philippines that was just recovering from the throes of war. Carlos was encouraged to seek a better future abroad and was told of jobs available on bases in Guam and Okinawa. He chose to go to the latter. With only an elementary education, Carlos had to be relegated to lesser-skilled jobs, but he chose to see it as an opportunity to learn more skills.

Enrico's case meanwhile, illustrates those who are part of the lower-middle class to middle-class groups who were able to receive a college education and the necessary cultural capital to be able to work in jobs that call for more skills, such as that of a musician. As I mentioned at the beginning of this chapter, Enrico was an electrical engineering student who was contracted to play on base in Japan as a jazz band member. Despite not finishing his engineering degree as he decided to stay on in Okinawa from 1958 (after a short stint playing on U.S. bases in Korea) to the present, it cannot be denied that Enrico's musical skills provided him with much cultural capital that enabled him to work as a musician even up to his 80s, where he teaches music and guitar to children of U.S. military personnel on Camp Foster since 2004. He also told me that during the post-war years, musicians were considered as officers, since they were highly regarded. James Roberson (2011) talks about how in the 1950s and 1960s in Okinawa, most of the musicians playing in clubs catering to American servicemen were Filipinos (Roberson 2011: 598). Musical skills can be translated into cultural capital in this regard, and playing music is not necessarily the same as working in the mess hall, kitchen, or in construction, and other such jobs that require manual labour. Enrico originally thought of staying only for two years in Okinawa and going back to Manila to finish his studies, but realized that what he would earn after graduating from university was not comparable to what he was earning in Okinawa as a musician. This apparently is caused by inequalities in the world system, then and now, wherein the pursuit of economic mobility and (economic) capital accumulation becomes more achievable (in a short amount of time) through migration. He then told me that he never regretted his decision.

As TCN work includes a whole hierarchy of occupations from the low-skilled to the highly professional class, it cannot be denied that within the category of TCN, inequalities also exist; not only among and within occupational status, but also among nationalities and ethnicities, as illustrated in the previous pages by the uneven pay-scale that pitted Filipinos with mainland Japanese, both considered TCNs during the Occupation of Okinawa.

Looking at the status of these TCNs in Okinawa, I argue that they are positioned as an "Other" to the Americans, as well as an "Other" to the local population. Thus, they can also be considered "occupiers" in themselves, as they were also allies of the Americans, albeit not being covered by Status of Forces Agreement (SOFA), which also points to less (job) security for the TCNs. Moreover, as an "Occupying Other" (Zulueta 2017), these Filipino TCNs may be considered to be a "site of American colonialism writ small" and we should not forget the fact that they were also ranked and paid higher wages than the Japanese and the Okinawans.

Stratification and Racialization of Base Work in Occupied Okinawa

As I pointed out in Chap. 2, the difference between Okinawans and the Japanese (that is, Japanese mainlanders) was strongly emphasized during the Occupation Period when General MacArthur was said to have stated that the "Okinawans are not Japanese" (Tomiyama 1990: 1; Nomura 2005: 28). This can be considered as a racist ploy that labelled Okinawans as the "Other"—and thus, inferior—to the erstwhile U.S. enemy, the Japanese. The underlying racism during this period was also manifested in base work, where Okinawans as LNs were situated on the lowest rank in the hierarchy (below the Japanese) of not only wage levels (as seen in the previous section), but also of type of work.

I also mentioned earlier that the number of TCNs was significantly reduced in the late 1950s, with their numbers only amounting to 4.2 per cent of the total civilian labour force (Yu-Jose 2002: 112). This reduction did not sit well with the Filipinos who decried the termination of their contracts as an issue of "persecution and discrimination" (Letters to the Editor, Morning Star 1957). Among the several documents I gathered from the Okinawa Prefectural Archives, a six-page letter written by Filipino returnees to the Department of Foreign Affairs in Manila in 1957 caught my attention. The letter was written by two former TCNs who identified themselves as members of the "Filipino Returnees from Okinawa Association". In it they outlined nine individual cases of discrimination and injustice towards Filipino TCNs despite "more than ten long years of loyal and faithful service to the United States Armed Forces in the Ryukyu Islands" (Letter to the Department of Foreign Affairs in Manila, 22 July 1957: 1). Most of the cases were about Filipino TCNs being terminated from their jobs (even before the end of contract), "bumped-off and separated from his job to accommodate an American civilian employee", and "forcibly" deported and repatriated. The letter also added that the "campaign of persecutions and discriminations is aimed only to (sic) the Filipinos and does not affect other nationals such as the Americans, Japanese or Chinese" (Ibid). While these cases undeniably illustrate underlying racisms within the context of base work, it also indicates that recruitment of base labour was (and is) highly gendered as it was racial, and that a "hierarchy of masculinities" (Eichler 2014: 607) among the workers and the TCNs (who were majority male) existed.

Meanwhile, upon the reversion of Okinawa to mainland Japan in 1972, changes regarding the employment of TCNs on U.S. military installations in the prefecture were evident. According to a telegram sent by the U.S. Department of State from the U.S. Embassy in Tokyo to the U.S. Embassy in Manila dated June 1972, TCNs on Okinawa before the reversion were under the jurisdiction of the United States, however with the prefecture's reversion to Japan, the presence of the U.S. Forces in the country is now under the terms of the U.S.-Japan Status of Forces

Agreement (SOFA), which makes no provisions for employment of TCNs, according to a telegram from the U.S. Embassy in Tokyo to its counterpart in Manila.[5] This document also states that before the reversion, TCN residence and employment in Okinawa was "completely" under U.S. jurisdiction. Thus, TCNs would have to be repatriated to their own countries upon receipt of severance pay. However, a TCN who has become a legal resident could opt to be hired by the USFJ command under a Master Labour Contract (MLC) or an Indirect Hire Agreement (IHA), wherein the Government of Japan now becomes the employer, at which wages and employment practices would be applicable as if the employee were a Japanese national (Telegram from Tokyo to Manila, June 1972, U.S. Department of State). Carlos also echoed this, when he shared that with the entry of the U.S.-Japan SOFA, "all Filipinos (and foreign nationals) will be terminated". He then added that he was told by the military, "you have to go, even though we need you".

Cries of discrimination were again heard from Filipino TCNs who denounced the unjust payment of severance benefits to them. According to the Department of Labour in Manila, an anonymous letter from a Filipino TCN based in Okinawa alleged acts of U.S. discrimination against Filipino workers in favour of Okinawan workers. It was alleged that Filipino TCNs will receive severance pay benefits of only a half month's pay for every year of service while Okinawan workers will receive an equivalent of a month's pay for every year of service (Telegram from Manila to Tokyo, U.S. Department of State, June 1972). It would be intriguing to note the changes in the treatment of both LNs (Okinawan workers) and TCNs (Filipino workers) in this regard and how shifts in economic privileges (in terms of remuneration and benefits) may also indicate shifts in racial and gendered hierarchies that are seen to continue at present. These shifts in hierarchies are also related to (current) state-level relations, in this case, U.S.-Japan relations, in the region, where economically advanced nations are given more privilege and status than those countries in the periphery.

It should also be noted here that Okinawa's relation to the United States and Japan has become "feminized", where occupied Okinawa is seen to be female (Molasky 1999), with the sexual violence and rape cases symbolic of Okinawa's victimhood to both Japanese (for allowing around 70 per cent of the U.S. bases on Okinawan soil) and American hegemony (the Occupation and the presence military bases) to this day (Angst 2009: 142). Likewise, Okinawans can also be seen as "feminized", with most of them relegated to low-skilled and unskilled work—that is, skilled work is equated to being "masculine", while unskilled work equals "feminine".

The roles played by the U.S. government and U.S. corporations in the recruitment of TCNs to these military bases are largely overlooked as much emphasis is given to people who are seen to migrate for greener pastures. These individuals are seen as solely pursuing their own economic gains—while this is most of the time true, the invisible hand of the United States and its "aggressive" role played through "colonialism, imperialist wars and occupations, capital investment and material extraction in Third World countries and through active recruitment of racialized and gendered immigrant labor" (Espiritu 2008: 207) escapes attention.

As I previously mentioned, most of these Filipino TCNs married or cohabited with Okinawan women, producing half-Okinawan and half-Filipino offspring. The existence of "mixed-race" Okinawans has not escaped academic attention (Noiri 2007; Shimabuku 2019), particularly when one talks of the Amerasian; and this issue has been increasingly significant in Okinawa's present as it was during its post-war years. In the next chapter, I talk about the offspring of these Filipino TCNs and Okinawan women, their identity formation as "mixed", or "hāfu", and how they can be considered as an "Other" to the Amerasian, a group borne out of intermarriages between U.S. servicemen and Asian women.

Notes

1. Foreign Service National.
2. During fieldwork in Okinawa in 2012, I personally met a Filipino female dentist—Dr Santos (pseudonym) who has been based in Okinawa since the immediate post-war years. She moved to Okinawa with her Filipino husband, also a dentist, to work on base during the Occupation Period. At the time of conversation, she lives with her son and daughter-in-law in Ginowan City. She still maintains her Filipino nationality.
3. Airgram from the U.S. Department of State to Manila, 27 February 1967.
4. General Headquarters, Far East Command, Adjutant General's Office Radio and Cable Center, Message from CG PHILRYCOM (Philippines-Ryukyus Command), 8 January 1947.
5. Telegram from U.S. Embassy Tokyo to U.S. Embassy Manila on the Filipino Employees on Okinawa, June 1972.

References

Amemiya, K. (1996, October 25). The Bolivian Connection: U.S. Bases and Okinawan Emigration. *Japan Policy Research Institute Working Paper no. 25.* http://wwws.jpri.org/publications/workingpapers/wp25.html. Accessed 10 Oct 2018

Angst, L. I. (2009). The Sacrifice of a Schoolgirl: The 1995 Rape Case, Discourses of Power, and Women's Lives in Okinawa. In L. M. Cuklanz & S. Moorti (Eds.), *Local Violence, Global Media: Feminist Analyses of Gendered Representations* (pp. 132–159). New York: Peter Lang Publishing, Inc.

Barker, I. V. (2009). (Re)Producing American Soldiers in an Age of Empire. *Politics and Gender, 5,* 211–235.

Eichler, M. (2014). Citizenship and the Contracting Out of Military Work: From National Conscription to Globalized Recruitment. *Citizenship Studies, 18*(6–7), 600–614.

Enloe, C. (2000). *Bananas, Beaches, and Bases: Making Feminist Sense of International Politics.* Berkeley: University of California Press.

Espiritu, Y. L. (2008). *Homebound: Filipino American Lives across Cultures, Communities, and Countries* (Philippine ed.). Quezon City: Ateneo de Manila University Press.

Letters to the Editor. *Morning Star,* 15 September 1957.

Lutz, C. (2009). *The Bases of Empire: the Global Struggle Against U.S. Military Posts.* New York: New York University Press.

Molasky, M. S. (1999). *The American occupation of Japan and Okinawa: Literature and Memory.* London: Routledge.

Nagumo, K. (1996). *Beigun Kichi to Rōdō Undō.* Kyoto: Kabushikigaisha Kamogawa Shuppan.

Noiri, N. (2007). Two Worlds: The Amerasian and the Okinawan. In J. Chinen (Ed.), *Uchinaanchu Diaspora: Memories, Continuities, Constructions (Social Processes in Hawaii)* (pp. 211–230). Honolulu: University of Hawaii Press.

Nomura, K. (2005). *Muishiki no Shokuminchishugi: Nihonjin no Beigunkichi to Okinawajin.* Tokyo: Ochanomizu Shobō.

Ohno, S. (1991). *Hapon: Firipin Nikkeijin no Nagai Sengo.* Tokyo: Daisan Shokan.

Pratt, M. L. (1992). *Imperial Eyes: Travel Writing and Transculturation.* London: Routledge.

Roberson, J. E. (2011). Doin' Our Thing: Identity and Colonial Modernity in Okinawan Rock Music. *Popular Music and Society, 34*(5), 593–620.

Sellek, Y. (2003). Migration and the Nation-State: Structural Explanations for Emigration from Okinawa. In G. D. Hook & R. Siddle (Eds.), *Japan and Okinawa: Structure and Subjectivity* (pp. 74–92). London: Routledge.

Shimabuku, A. M. (2019). *Alegal: Biopolitics and the Unintelligibility of Okinawan Life.* New York: Fordham University Press.

Suzuki, N., & Tamaki, S. (1996). Okinawa no Firipinjin: Teijūsha toshite mata Gaikokujin Rōdōsha toshite. *Ryukyu Hōgaku, 57*, 88–61.
Tobaru, T. A. (1998). *Ethnic and National Filipinos in Okinawa: A Descriptive Study of Their Way of Life and Patterns of Cultural Adaptation*. Unpublished M.A. Thesis, University of the Philippines.
Tomiyama, I. (1990). *Kindai Nihon Shakai to "Okinawajin": Nihonjin ni naru to iu koto*. Tokyo: Nihon Keizai Hyōronsha.
United States Department of State Unclassified Document on TCNs. http://www.state.gov/documents/organization/85316.pdf
USAID Foreign Service National Personnel Administration, ADS Chapter 495:13. http://www.usaid.gov/sites/default/files/documents/1877/495.pdf
Yoshida, K. (2001). *Democracy Betrayed: Okinawa Under U.S. Occupation*. Bellingham: Centre for East Asian Studies, Western Washington University.
Yoshida, K. (2007). *"Gunji Shokuminchi" Okinawa: Nihon Hondo to no "Ondosa" no Shōtai*. Tokyo: Kōbunken.
Yu-Jose, L. N. (2002). *Filipinos in Japan and Okinawa, 1880s–1972*. Tokyo: Research Institute for the Languages and Cultures of Asia and Africa, Tokyo University of Foreign Studies.
Zulueta, J. O. (2017). The Occupying Other: Third-Country Nationals and the U.S. Bases in Okinawa. In P. Iacobelli & H. Matsuda (Eds.), *Rethinking Postwar Okinawa: Beyond American Occupation* (pp. 39–57). Lanham: Lexington Books.

CORRESPONDENCE DATA

General Headquarters, Far East Command, Adjutant General's Office Radio and Cable Center, Message from CG PHILRYCOM (Philippines-Ryukyus Command), 8 January 1947 (Declassified: 20 August 1975).
Letter to the Department of Foreign Affairs in Manila, 22 July 1957. Department of Foreign Affairs Records.
National Archives and Research Administration, U.S.A.: USCAR (United States Civil Administration of the Ryukyus), Box 1279, Entry 1613: Airgram from the U.S. Department of State to Manila, 27 February 1967.
Recruitment of Filipino Laborers and Employees by the United States Army, Treaties and International Acts Series 3646, Agreement Between the United States of America and the Republic of the Philippines, Effected by Exchange of Notes, Signed at Manila, May 13 and 16, 1947. U.S. Department of State.
United States of America Department of State. Telegram from American Embassy in Tokyo to American Embassy in Manila (Subject: U.S. Forces Filipino Employees on Okinawa), June 1972. Box 1791, F3.

CHAPTER 4

The "Other" Mixed Race: The Nisei in Perspective

Studies on people of Okinawan descent in the South East Asian, particularly in the Philippine, context are scant, and if at least they appear in literature on migration and/or ethnic studies, they are usually subsumed under the broader category of *Nikkeijin* or *Nikkei* (a person of Japanese descent). Yamashita Yasuko also mentions that studies about Okinawan migrants to the United States have been subsumed under those of the *Nikkei-Amerikajin* or Americans of Japanese descent (Yamashita 2007: 87–89). Though treated as "the Other" by mainland Japanese immigrants, she said that these Okinawan migrants were overlooked in studies of Japanese-Americans. It was only in the 1980s, upon the publication of the book *Uchinanchu* (Okinawans), by the University of Hawaii in 1981, that studies of Okinawan immigrants in the United States began to take root (Ibid: 90).

However, these people's ancestry as Okinawans or *Uchinānchu*—in the Okinawan "dialect" or *hōgen*—indicates their unique history decades past when Okinawa flourished as the Kingdom of the Ryukyus, thus speaking of a distinct identity for these island people. The role that Okinawa played as an emigrant society in pre-war Japanese history, as well as its role as host to U.S. military installations in post-war Japan, suggests that Okinawa ought to be considered significant in itself. In this regard, the out- and in-migrations that occurred in Okinawa since the immediate post-war years deserve to be accorded attention as these movements are also intertwined with current issues on immigration and the U.S.-Japan Security Treaty, not to mention the current base issues in Okinawa.

© The Author(s) 2020
J. O. Zulueta, *Transnational Identities on Okinawa's Military Bases*,
https://doi.org/10.1007/978-981-32-9787-6_4

In this chapter, I discuss the identity construction of the Nisei and how they see themselves in relation to other people of part-Okinawan or part-Japanese descent. I indicate how Nisei became an identity marker in itself for this group of "half-Okinawan", "half-Filipino" individuals. I also locate the discussion of being "half-Japanese", or "hāfu" within the context of "mixed" identities in Okinawa.

Issei, Nisei, Sansei

Within *Nikkeijin* communities, generational categories are usually used to classify members. The first-generation Japanese emigrants are called *issei*, and is conventionally used to refer to the immigrant generation who emigrated mostly as *dekasegi* or migrant workers, and have settled in their host countries, making these their homes. The second generation or *nisei* refers to the offspring of first-generation immigrants; the first generation born in the host country. The *sansei* or third generation is the offspring of the second generation, the fourth (*yonsei*), the offspring of the third, the fifth (*gosei*), the offspring of the fourth, and so on. The *issei* are usually considered to be Japanese, while their descendants, who mostly took on the citizenship of their natal country, are indicated by the category, *Nikkei* or *Nikkeijin*.

However, what is interesting with this group of Okinawans who moved to the Philippines is their use of these generational categories that pertain not necessarily to their experience of migration, but to descent, that is, their Okinawan lineage. As I mentioned in Chap. 1, the term Nisei—which I use throughout this book with an uppercase "N"—has become an identity marker that these half-Okinawan, half-Filipinos use to identify themselves. Thus, the general categories of *issei*, *nisei*, and *sansei* are not being used according to what convention dictates, but rather are largely used within in-group situations and are largely self-ascribed. Moreover, there is emphasis on heritage and "blood", starting from the so-called Nisei, who are characterized by a mixed Filipino and Okinawan parentage. Therefore, *issei* refers to the Okinawan parent, *nisei* refers to the offspring of the *issei* to a Filipino spouse (whether that *nisei* was born in Okinawa or elsewhere), and *sansei* refers to the offspring of the *nisei* (regardless whether the *nisei*'s spouse is a fellow *nisei* or not). This particular classification of the *nisei* was also used by Ohno Shun (1992: 5–6):

Offspring of Okinawan women and Filipino men who worked in Okinawa in U.S. military installations during the allied occupation of Japan and Okinawa during the 1950s to the 1960s—these include those who were born and raised in Okinawa who eventually settled in the Philippines, as well as those who were already born in the Philippines (emphasis, mine).

Hence, this self-ascription as Nisei among these people with both Okinawan and Filipino parentage points to an identity that they have constructed among themselves, vis-à-vis other people of Japanese (including Okinawan) and Filipino heritage. In the following section, I discuss more about how the Nisei identity has been constructed.

Understanding the Nisei: Migrations and Ethnic Group Formation

The concept of the "Nisei" here is to be looked at as an identity marker that is primarily a self-ascribed category used largely within in-group situations. Based on earlier fieldwork and correspondence with the Philippine Okinawan Society (*Firipin Okinawa Kenjinkai*) or POS, I found out that *issei, nisei*, and *sansei* are categories used within the organization to refer to the Okinawan women, their children, and grandchildren, respectively. This usage apparently does not conform to studies of Japanese immigrants where *issei* refers to the immigrant generation, and *nisei* points to the first generation born in the host country (e.g. see Tsuda's studies on the Brazilian Nikkeijin (2003) and Nakano Glenn's work on Japanese-American women (1986)). As the category of Nisei I use here is largely self-ascribed, there is no doubt—as I mentioned at the beginning of this chapter—that emphasis is given to "blood". Thus, *issei, nisei*, and *sansei*, point to consanguinity ("blood relation"), rather than the period or time of migration. The Nisei also describe themselves as "half", particularly to people outside the group. As previously mentioned, these individuals are offspring of Okinawan women and Filipino men. The Filipinos worked on base as professionals, skilled and semi-skilled workers, and soldiers (i.e. Philippine Scouts) under the USCAR (United States Civil Administration of the Ryukyus) government during the Allied Occupation of the prefecture (Tobaru 1998: 31; Yu Jose 2002: 117). Up until 1954, these marriages were estimated to be around 1054 (Sugii 2009: 45).

It should be noted that the creation of this particular ethnic group can be traced to larger socio-political and socio-economic factors that spurred migrations between Okinawa and the Philippines in both the pre-war and post-war years. It was largely due to the demand for labour by the U.S. Occupation Forces in Okinawa that brought about these migrations, and with it, the reproduction of the second generation that would eventually take on jobs on base, reminiscent of their fathers. Thus, it can be said that the Nisei is an ethnic group historically constructed largely due to the American Occupation of Okinawa and is a by-product of migrations within this region in the post-war years; in particular, between Okinawa and the Philippines.

Thousands of Nisei were born in Okinawa.[1] Of these, some were raised in the Philippines, while others were raised in Okinawa and eventually moved to the Philippines when they were adolescents. There were also those who were born and raised in the Philippines. The move to the Philippines was precipitated when the work contracts of their Filipino fathers expired, whereas there were also cases when the Filipinos were sent back to the Philippines before the expiry of their contracts without being given clear reasons for it, as I mentioned in the previous chapter. Filipino workers decried the act as discriminatory and some of them filed charges. There were cases wherein the Filipino husband left his Okinawan wife and child in Okinawa, and no contact was ever made upon the husband's return to the Philippines. Thus, these Nisei only have vague memories of their father. An illustration of this is a novel written by a Nisei who travelled to Manila in search of his father (See Sunamori 2000).

These Nisei were born during the immediate post-war years and most of them are currently in their mid-50s to late-60s. Most of these individuals reside in the Philippines, and a majority of them live in Metropolitan Manila or the so-called National Capital Region (which is the area surrounding Metropolitan Manila).[2] They have stable jobs; most are highly educated (with at least a college degree), and belong to the middle to upper-middle class in Philippine society. Some are entrepreneurs and travel between Okinawa and the Philippines to conduct their businesses. However, it cannot be denied that several of these Nisei, especially those located in rural areas and more peripheral regions in the country, are not as blessed. Membership in the POS enabled the Nisei to be in touch with their fellow Nisei, the *issei* (the Okinawan mothers), and the third generation of the *sansei*, as well as with their Okinawan roots. The POS is the first and the biggest Okinawan association in post-war South East Asia. Founded in

1982 by a group of Philippine-based Okinawan businessmen and young Okinawan students studying in Philippine universities, it was created to "cultivate mutual friendships among the Okinawans in the Philippines and further their well-being; promote international exchange especially in the fields of culture and education; and deepen mutual understanding between the people of two cultures" (Evangelista 2002: 6). The organization served as a venue that enabled *issei* women to get-together and socialize during monthly meetings.

It cannot be denied that like most so-called mixed identities, the Nisei identity is diverse. This identity marker also differs in degree and definition amongst the Nisei themselves, as this specific identity suggests a degree of "shuttling" from one ethnic identification to another, between being Filipino and being Okinawan. The Nisei then is:

> characteristically able to shuttle to and from one ethnic identity to another— that of being Okinawan and Filipino—while still remaining a Nisei... their shuttling involves identifying with either ethnic identity, since for them, there is no greater identity... [T]hey are equally Okinawan and Filipino. (Zulueta 2004: 69)

The Nisei emphasize both their roots, while claiming to be part of both Okinawa and the Philippines.

Moreover, these Nisei engage in boundary-making processes particularly when claiming a "half-Okinawan" identity, thereby distinguishing themselves from other so-called mixed identities in Japanese and Okinawan society, such as the Amerasians, the Philippine *Nikkeijin* (Japanese-Filipinos), and the so-called Japanese-Filipino Children/Youth (JFC/JFY), who are mostly offspring of Japanese men and Filipino women who came to Japan as workers and marriage migrants from the early 1980s. This claim to being "hāfu" can be regarded as a form and a source of empowerment for the Nisei as they negotiate their mixed ethnic identity with notions of being "Japanese"/ "Okinawan" in present-day Okinawan society. Holders of Japanese nationality, they are "Japanese" in a legal sense, but their being "half", coupled with their inadequate Japanese language proficiency and cultural literacy, as well as their "un-typical Japanese" mannerisms, contradicts what being "Japanese" is. The Nisei then exist between being "excluded" and "included" in the category of "Japanese". They are Japanese legally, culturally though they are not. For some of these Nisei, being Japanese is more of a legal identity. This, I realized, one Sunday in September

2013 while conversing with Noel Tōma, a Nisei parishioner at Oroku Catholic Church. When we were talking about his recent trip to the Philippines where he availed of senior citizen discounts by using his Filipino name, he then told me (after probably seeing a surprised look on my face), "*Sa papel lang ako Hapon (I am Japanese only on paper)*"—apparently suggesting the instrumentalist view he has on his Japanese nationality and how he locates himself within the category of being "Japanese".

For the Nisei, being "hāfu" is less about cultural markers, but more about consanguinity. The claim to being "hāfu" is, for many of them, an assertion of one's roots and "blood" relation to an Okinawan parent despite not exhibiting cultural traits of being "Okinawan". It can be said that this particular claim to an identity works to serve as cultural capital as well as a "passport" to be able to enter the Japanese labour market. This claim also enables them to craft a sense of belongingness in an Okinawa that is ambivalent towards people like them. I will be discussing this more in Chap. 5. Meanwhile, to understand further how "mixed" identities are perceived in Okinawan society, I turn to a short discussion on so-called hāfu identities and locate this within the discourse of racialization in Japan/Okinawa.

"Mixed" Identities in Contemporary Okinawa

The term "half", or its Japanized form, "hāfu", has been examined and problematized by numerous scholars looking at the reality of mixed ethnic identities in Japan. The word "hāfu" was said to have been used in Japan since the 1930s (Iwabuchi 2014: 11). Iwabuchi Koichi defines "hāfu" as a category of people that is racially classified, and are the products/offspring of the "racial mixing" of the historically constructed (category) of "Japanese (*Nihonjin*)" and "a different ethnic group (*iminzoku*)", "a different race (*ijinshu*)", or a "foreigner (*gaikokujin*)" (Ibid: 13). While a majority of the studies on the "hāfu" category of people in contemporary Japan focus on current perceptions about them in the media, the understanding and perception on "hāfu" in the immediate post-war years ought to be thought of in a different context, and this is where I contextualize the so-called half ethnic identity of the Nisei.

During the post-war years, Okinawa had its share of offspring from intercultural or "interracial" unions due mainly to military basing in the prefecture. At first, intermarriages were not legally allowed in Okinawa (Shimabuku 2010: 368). Along with issues of miscegenation, Okinawan women marrying or having relationships with the occupying forces were stigmatized and were seen to be working as "prostitutes" (Zulueta 2017: 553). This same information was also shared to me by Yagi Tsunekazu, president of the Okinawa-based, Okinawan-Filipino Association, when I first spoke to him in March 2010. Along with so-called Amerasians—whose presence in the prefecture cannot be denied due to their physical attributes that betray their "difference"—offspring of Okinawan women and Filipino men were born. According to reports by Uruma Shimpo, in September 1949, there were 150 mixed-blood Filipino births for three years (upon the time of reporting), in contrast to 273 Amerasians born in this period (of which 216 children were mixed-"white" and 57, mixed-"black"). However, the *Okinawa Times* reported statistics from the Naha Police Department covering the Naha, Oroku, Mawashi, and Minato districts,[3] and indicated 53 half-Filipino children, 21 half-"white", and 17 half-"black" (Shimabuku 2010: 368). Shimabuku adds that the mention of the existence of mixed-blood children was heavily censored and that a "deluge of information" about this was not released until 1952 (Ibid: 369). The article moreover states that of the 52 Okinawan mothers, two were married under Naha City jurisdiction, and 28 fathers had already returned to their countries (Ibid). Considering these attitudes towards "mixed" offspring in the post-war years, we can further understand their marginalized position in contemporary Okinawan society.

The "Other" to the Amerasian

To speak of the presence of the U.S. military in Okinawa and its relationship to the local community is almost tantamount to addressing issues such as intermarriages and the birth of these "mixed race" children, commonly known as "Amerasians". The term Amerasian points to the offspring of U.S. servicemen stationed in Asia and local Asian women. It was said to be first coined by writer Pearl S. Buck based on her experiences in China, in her novel *East Wind, West Wind*, published in 1930 (Valverde 1992: 144; Kutschera and Caputi 2012: 7). In Okinawa, Amerasians are a continuing legacy of the U.S. presence in the prefecture, where they continue to experience discrimination. Noiri Naomi discusses that in contemporary Okinawa, it is the Amerasian children that are more "visible" in society rather than the adult Amerasians who usually work in "less secure sectors" of the Okinawan economy—such as at nightclubs, cafes, restaurants, and on U.S. military bases as store clerks (Noiri 2007: 212).

While Noiri also calls Amerasians an "invisible, internal minority" (Noiri 2007: 211), I would like to note that physically, Amerasians are more different from the locals, owing to their "mixed" racial heritage—having either a "white" or a "black" father, and thus are more conspicuous. However, unlike Amerasians, these Nisei are not as physically noticeable—as both parents are of Asian heritage—and hence can be deemed to be more "invisible". This is due to the fact that the common perception of the term, "mixed race", is synonymous with a "black" and "white" mix (Mahtani and Moreno 2004: 313). These "non-white" and "non-black" mixed race people tend to be marginalized in current debates and discourses about the topic as the usual focus is on a "white-non-white" dichotomy, or a "white-black" dichotomy, or in some cases, a "black-non-black" one, thus overlooking "non-white/black"-"non-white/black" mixed peoples. While military basing "created" these Amerasians, it also created the "Others" to the Amerasians—that is, offspring of Asian women and "non-white" base workers, who in most cases were hired not necessarily to take on high-skilled jobs, but also semi-skilled or low-skilled ones. In Chap. 7, I elaborate on the Nisei's status as an "invisible minority" not only because of their physical attributes that do not betray their difference, but also because, even though they are Japanese nationals, they are not considered to fully belong in the category "Japanese", that more often than not, tends to conflate ethnicity, race, culture, and nationality.

In line with this "invisibility" I mentioned above, while previous studies on race looked at perceived physiological differences such as skin colour, one also has to note that there are disenfranchised groups that are not perceived to be physically different from the mainstream and yet "are treated as different kinds of human species by the dominant majorities" (Takezawa 2011: 8). Takezawa Yasuko argues for the need for a new understanding of "race" that takes into account experiences of groups outside the United States and Europe. She adds that "race", "results from an organized process of social differentiation and boundary making, often linked with conflicts of interest" (Takezawa 2011: 9). She further states that historical documents in Japan describe people such as the *burakumin* (a group ranked at the lowest level of the social hierarchy in feudal Japan) as people of a "different race (*jinshu ga chigau*)". In line with this, Kurokawa, in her analysis of *burakumin* representation in the film, *Hashi No Nai Kawa* (Part I—1969; Part II—1970), writes how race has been used to represent "innate and unalterable distinction", which, she argues, creates an "invisible race" (Kurokawa 2011: 45). It should be noted here that the *burakumin* are ethnically Japanese, but are considered "dirty" due to the occupations they had which dealt with dirt and death (such as butchers and undertakers).

In the case of Okinawans, they were primarily seen as ethnically and culturally different, to the extent that they had to be "civilized" and had to undergo a process of modernization to be part of the Japanese nation-state. Moreover, "being Okinawan" should be understood within the context and effects of Japanese colonialism as well as the U.S. Occupation of the prefecture which lasted for 20 more years than that of the mainland, as well as the continuing U.S. presence in the form of its military bases. On the one hand, Okinawa seems to be incorporated into the discourse of the Japanese "self" particularly when issues regarding security are at stake, while on the other hand, it reinforces the perception that Okinawans are different from the Japanese in that they are burdened with a "disproportionate responsibility" for the country's security with most of the bases existing on Okinawan soil (Allen 2002: 9). They are in a position where they are seen as both Japanese and not Japanese (*"Nihonjin" de atte "Nihonjin" de nai*) (Oguma 1998: 280). The same goes for people who are seen and see themselves as "mixed" and/or "half" or "hāfu" (half-Japanese/Okinawan), where they occupy an ambiguous position between being Japanese or not; and for those who trace their roots to Okinawa, being of "mixed race" challenges not only the notion of being Japanese, but also that of being Okinawan.

Being "half" or "mixed", in this case, being an offspring of an Okinawan and another Asian whose national membership is relatively lower in terms of economic standing, can invite discrimination from others. This, despite having Japanese nationality. In most cases, one's cultural differences and "foreignness" is given more emphasis. Raphael Miyagi, a former base worker (now retired) whom I mentioned in Chap. 1, shared: "you are never a Japanese, you are never an Okinawan; you're always a Filipino in the eyes of the people over here". Despite having Japanese nationality and an Okinawan mother, Raphael states that they are still seen as foreign, with more focus given to their non-Japanese/Okinawan parentage. This is also because these people are not considered "culturally" Japanese due to their low-level of Japanese proficiency (particularly in reading and writing) and to some extent, their unfamiliarity with some cultural norms. Thus, they are relegated to the "foreign" and "Other" category, belying their status as (legally) "Japanese".

Re-racialization in Japan/Okinawa

In this section, I examine the contemporary hierarchy/ies of mixed identities in Japan founded on perceived "racial" categories, which are mainly based on ethnic differences compounded by perceived economic hierarchies, based on unequal economic standings of countries in the world system. While racialization indicates categorization according to "race/s", and is the "process by which certain bodily features or assumed biological characteristics are used systematically to mark certain persons for differential status or treatment" (Cornell and Hartmann 1998: 33), I use the term, re-racialization here to point to the process whereby a person or a group has been (re)attributed another "racial" meaning or category that may have led to that person or group being considered in a more positive or negative light than before. I also highlight here the spatio-temporal factors that are significant in this process.

"Race" and racial categories have been used in many societies to mark people as having a different social status that is more or less tied to economic standing. In Japan, the "Other", which is deemed different in terms of physical features, skin colour, culture, and national membership, is seen as "inferior", whereas, people who are considered "white" and belong to the "West" are seen in a more favourable light. "Foreignness" as a category in Japan is racialized not only according to physical phenotype but also according to one's ethnic or national membership, thus creating a hierarchy of "Others" in a Japan that continues to see itself as homogeneous.

It should also be noted that "mixed" identities in Japan are also hierarchical where people of "mixed" Western or "white" parentage occupy the highest position, with Asians categorized below them. Even among Asians, hierarchies exist based on nationality, with people in economically less-developed regions ranked lower. Compounded by the peripheral position of the Philippines in the world system, as well as the migration streams from the Philippines to Japan in the early 1980s to the 1990s, which was mostly comprised of low-skilled workers and female "entertainers", Japanese/Okinawans with part-Filipino parentage, currently do not necessarily occupy a privileged position in the "mixed race hierarchy" as opposed to their part-white counterparts.

Space and Time in the Re-racialization of Mixed Identities

Here, I look at the temporal and spatial significance of racialization by looking at the case of these people with both Okinawan and Filipino parents. I support my observations and arguments with some narratives culled from informant interviews, by looking at three space-time frames: Okinawa in the early years of the Occupation, the Philippines in the immediate post-war years, and contemporary Okinawa (that is, post-reversion—1972—to the present).

As I discussed in Chap. 3, Filipinos were hired as TCNs to work on base construction as well as to staff these installations during the immediate post-war years. While seen as an "Other" and part of the Occupation forces, the Filipinos were positioned at a higher level in the base hierarchy, as they were paid higher wages in contrast to the Japanese and Okinawans. It was also said that for many women during this time, marriage with Americans and members of the Allied Forces was a way out of extreme conditions that left post-war Okinawa a desolate place. The early years of the Occupation period saw several intermarriages between Okinawan women and foreign men, despite these being not fully accepted by the locals. This was also related to issues of miscegenation.

When the contracts of their fathers were terminated, the Nisei joined their parents on the return to the Philippines. The move to the Philippines also had its challenges, as for one, most of these Filipino TCNs were not necessarily members of privileged classes back in their home country. Some were even from far-flung provinces, and were originally farmers. While their Okinawan wives experienced several challenges in adjustment to life in the Philippines, their children had to do so as well. Upon relocation to the Philippines, these Nisei attended local schools and interacted with Filipino classmates. However, Philippine sentiments against the Japanese were still ripe during the immediate post-war years, and some of the Nisei would talk about how they were bullied or how they got into fights. "I was always getting into fights because of my identity," Raphael once told me. To be Japanese or part-Japanese was to be an enemy in the early post-war years in the Philippines. Meryl Miyazato, told me that when she was growing up in the Philippines, she also experienced discrimination. She, however, did not elaborate on this. Back in 2003, I spoke to

Eric, who was based in Manila (he remained in Manila after he and his parents moved from Okinawa when he was ten), and he spoke of unpleasant experiences he had then in Manila. He spoke to me about being challenged to a fight and how his classmates in school would even throw stones at him and hurl curses at him.

Being born to Okinawan women, who were seen to be no different from the mainland Japanese by the Filipinos during that time, quite a number of Nisei experienced discrimination for being a child of a *Haponesa* (Japanese woman). Raphael adds, "nobody knows about Okinawa. Even my dad, when he came over (to Okinawa), he didn't know where Okinawa was. They only knew that they were going to Japan." He also said that people rarely knew about Okinawa as there was little mention of Okinawa in history books.

Post-reversion Okinawa saw the prefecture as part of a Japan that has recovered from the throes of war and was gaining ground to be one of the largest economies in the world. Japan in the 1980s was experiencing its fast-growth years, known as the "bubble" years. This period also saw the beginning of the return migration of these Nisei to their birthplace—with some of them returning as early as the 1970s. It should be stated here though that this period preceded the deployment of Filipino workers to Japan and that these Nisei were mostly "individual" migrants, returning for reasons such as the acquisition of a Japanese nationality, economic and career mobility, and to "be in touch" with their identity as part-Okinawans (Zulueta 2012). However, Raphael told me that in Okinawa, "there's always gonna be discrimination, it doesn't matter just because you are half." Meryl echoes this when she spoke of how she is also looked at as a foreigner:

> I think their first impression, they think I'm an Okinawan, but when I start speaking Japanese, it's chotto hen (a little strange) [laughter]. You know, the accent is different, or it's grammatically incorrect, or there's this hesitancy in explaining things in Japanese, so you'll be looked at as a foreigner.

In the post-reversion years (from 1972), Filipinos in Japan and Okinawa were not considered to occupy a more privileged position (as what was reflective of the base work hierarchy during the immediate post-war years) as Filipinos began arriving in Japan as so-called entertainers (who mostly worked in pubs and bars) and low-skilled workers working mostly in factories and the construction sector. While Japan has become one of the most economically powerful countries in the world system, the Philippines in the 1980s was experiencing political instability and economic woes, and since then was relegated to its current third-world status. Thus, being Filipino in Japan was equated with that of being a low-skilled worker, contributing to a "re-racialization" of the Filipino, and in effect, a "re-racialization" also of those people who are "half"-Filipino, like the Nisei.

The ethnic category of "Japanese" as well as the legal category of "Japanese" as nationality are, on the whole, tied to the myth of homogeneity of which the conflation of race, ethnicity, and people is very much implied. The conception of pre-war citizenship and nationality in imperial Japan included ethnically different subjects, such as the Taiwanese and Koreans, who were under the emperor. During the post-war era, however, membership in the Japanese nation-state has come to be defined in terms of consanguinity under the Japanese emperor (Chung 2010: 70), hence ethnically different people are excluded. Therefore, for the so-called half or hāfu, theirs is an existence that is defined between exclusion and inclusion in this whole category of being "Japanese"; a presence that is also between being included and excluded in Japanese and Okinawan society.

Notes

1. The exact number of Nisei born in Okinawa is difficult to get hold of due to the fact that no records of registration exist in the Philippine Consulate in Okinawa.
2. As of 2003, the membership list of the Philippine Okinawan Society lists around 1000 plus of its Nisei members as living in Metropolitan Manila (other members reside in the outskirts). When I was conducting this research, I used to visit the POS office for updates, but was told that the membership list still needs to be updated and the person-in-charge of the POS office (i.e. the secretary) could not give me a more updated members' directory. The office secretary also told me that there were some Nisei members in the list who migrated to Okinawa. Since 2016, the POS office located in Quezon City in Metropolitan Manila is now closed. However, the organization still exists and the officers occasionally hold meetings at designated places, such as a member's house.
3. These three districts are now part of Naha City.

References

Allen, M. (2002). *Identity and Resistance in Okinawa*. Lanham: Rowman & Littlefield Publishers, Inc.

Chung, E. A. (2010). *Immigration and Citizenship in Japan*. New York: Cambridge University Press.

Cornell, S., & Hartmann, D. (1998). *Ethnicity and Race: Making Identities in a Changing World*. Thousand Oaks: Pine Forge Press.

Evangelista, M. H. (2002). The Philippine Okinawa Society Comes of Age. In *20th Anniversary Program and Directory of the Philippine-Okinawan Society*. Quezon City: Philippine Okinawan Society.

Iwabuchi, K. (2014). *Hāfu to wa Dare ka?: Jinshu Konkō, Media Hyōshō, Kōshō Jissen*. Tokyo: Seikyusha.

Kurokawa, M. (2011). Markers of the "Invisible Race": On the Film Hashi No Nai Kawa. In Y. Takezawa (Ed.), *Racial Representations in Asia* (pp. 32–52). Kyoto/Melbourne: Kyoto University Press and Trans Pacific Press.

Kutschera, P. C., & Caputi, M. A. (2012). *The Case for Categorization of Military Filipino Amerasians as Diaspora*. Paper presented at 9th International Conference on the Philippines (ICOPHIL-9). Michigan State University, E. Lansing, MI. http://www.amerasianresearch.org/pdf/ICOPHIL-9FINALFilipinoDiaspora-Kutschera-Caputi.pdf. Accessed 30 Apr 2019.

Mahtani, M., & Moreno, A. (2004). Same Difference: Towards a More Unified Discourse in "Mixed Race" Theory. In J. O. Ifekwunigwe (Ed.), *Mixed Race Studies: A Reader* (pp. 313–317). London: Routledge.

Nakano Glenn, E. (1986). *Issei, Nisei, War Bride: Three Generations of Japanese American Women in Domestic Service*. Philadelphia: Temple University Press.

Noiri, N. (2007). Two Worlds: The Amerasian and the Okinawan. In J. Chinen (Ed.), *Uchinanchu Diaspora: Memories, Continuities, and Constructions (Social Processes in Hawaii)* (pp. 211–230). Honolulu: University of Hawaii Press.

Oguma, E. (1998). *"Nihonjin" no Kyōkai: Okinawa, Ainu, Taiwan, Chōsen Shokuminchi Shihai kara Fukki Undō made*. Tokyo: Shinyōsha.

Ohno, S. (1992). *Japanese-Filipinos in Davao: A Preliminary Study of an Ethnic Minority*. Unpublished M.A. Thesis, University of the Philippines.

Shimabuku, A. (2010). Petitioning Subjects: Miscegenation in Okinawa from 1945 to 1952 and the Crisis of Sovereignty. *Inter-Asia Cultural Studies, 11*(3), 355–374.

Sugii, M. (2009). Beigun Tōchika Okinawa ni okeru Firipin-jin e no Manazashi: Sengo 12-nen kan no shinbun kiji wo moto ni. *Okinawa Kenkyū Nōto* (18), 41–59.

Sunamori, K. (2000). *Okinawa Shauto*. Tokyo: Kodansha.

Takezawa, Y. (Ed.). (2011). *Racial Representations in Asia*. Kyoto and Melbourne: Kyoto University Press and Trans Pacific Press.

Tobaru, T. A. (1998). *Ethnic and National Filipinos in Okinawa: A Descriptive Study of Their Way of Life and Patterns of Cultural Adaptation*. Unpublished M.A. Thesis, University of the Philippines.

Tsuda, T. (2003). *Strangers in the Ethnic Homeland: Japanese Brazilian Return Migration in Transnational Perspective*. New York: Columbia University Press.

Valverde, C. K. (1992). From Dust to Gold: The Vietnamese Amerasian Experience. In M. P. P. Root (Ed.), *Racially Mixed People in America* (pp. 144–161). Newbury Park: Sage Publications.

Yamashita, Y. (2007). "Okinawakei Imin" Kenkyū no Tenkai to Shiza. In T. Iyotani (Ed.), *Idō kara Basho e To: Gendai Imin Kenkyū no Kadai* (pp. 85–105). Tokyo: Yushindo Kōbunsha.

Yu Jose, L. N. (2002). *Filipinos in Japan and Okinawa (1880s–1972)*. Tokyo: Research Institute for the Languages and Cultures of Asia and Africa, Tokyo University of Foreign Studies.

Zulueta, J. O. (2004). The Nisei: The Second-Generation Okinawan-Filipinos in Metro Manila. *Philippine Sociological Review, 52*, 55–74.

Zulueta, J. O. (2012). Living as Migrants in a Place That Was Once "Home": The Nisei, the U.S. Bases, and Okinawan Society. *Philippine Studies: Historical and Ethnographic Viewpoints, 60*(3), 367–390.

Zulueta, J. O. (2017). An Invisible Minority? Return Migration and Ethnicity in Okinawa. *Social Identities: Journal for the Study of Race, Nation and Culture, 23*(5), 548–561.

CHAPTER 5

The Return to Okinawa: Capital, Networks, Mobility

THE CONCEPT OF RETURN IN MIGRATION

A return in the migration process is usually considered to be an "end", whereby the migrant sees himself/herself as fulfilling his/her purpose/s for migration, which is usually economic, and thus the return to one's homeland signals the end of the migration itself. In other cases, a return points to a "failure" on the part of the migrant to realize his/her goals for migration and thus the decision to return becomes imminent. However, return, as an "integral part of the migration experience" (Long and Oxfeld 2004: 2–3), should not be seen as "an end in the migration cycle" as it "constitutes one stage in the migration process" (Cassarino 2004: 268).

Nevertheless, is it still viable to talk about return in a world very much in flux, and here I echo Xiang Biao when he asks whether it still makes sense to talk about return migration when movements are "multi-directional, identity is replaced by hybridity, the local community is entangled with transnational space, and 'home' and 'away' are both destabilized and the division between are blurred" (Xiang 2014: 167)? As opposed to earlier theories on return migration that considers return as fixed, such that the return is seen to be either a failure of the migrant in the host country (neoclassical economics) or a success on the part of the migrant that enables him/her to return as he/she meets his/her objectives for migrating (new economics of labour migration), transnationalism and the social network theory perspectives view return as not fixed or "permanent" and as such, is just a step in the whole migration project (Cassarino 2004: 269).

© The Author(s) 2020
J. O. Zulueta, *Transnational Identities on Okinawa's Military Bases*,
https://doi.org/10.1007/978-981-32-9787-6_5

On the other hand, scholars also talk about an ethnic "return", whereby the migrant is returning to his/her ancestral land—to which the migrant only knows as a far-away place and the subject of his/her grandparents' stories. In his study on Japanese-Brazilians in Japan, Takeyuki Tsuda (2009) defines "*ethnic* return migration" (emphasis included in the original), to point to the "later-generation descendants of diasporic peoples who 'return' to their countries of ancestral origin after living outside their ethnic homelands for generations" (Tsuda 2009: 1). Japanese-Brazilian return migrants are ethnic return migrants in a sense as they were already born and brought up in Brazil and thus the return to their ancestral homeland (i.e. Japan) is tied more to feelings of "nostalgia rather than by realistic experience" (Piore 1979: 119). It is also linked to economic and financial reasons and the fact that wages in Japan are relatively much higher than what they earn back in Brazil.

This chapter looks at adult[1] return migration from the Philippines to Okinawa that has been occurring since the 1970s. Much of these returns were happening on an individual level and thus, as opposed to the large-scale return migration of Japanese-Brazilians in the 1990s, these returns were not as conspicuous. I also examine the Nisei's return process/es and perceptions of home, which is very much linked to both capital ownership (i.e. cultural and social) and capital accumulation (i.e. economic and symbolic).

I also aim to utilize the concept of return or return migration as a heuristic device in analysing and understanding capital, home, and migration among return migrants in Okinawa. Inherent in its term as movement or motion, returns arguably provide one with the tools necessary in understanding and analysing the concept of home in migration as well as the role capital (i.e. economic, cultural, and social capital) plays in this whole process. I argue that the concept of return in this regard is primarily actor-led (despite the palpable role of the state in border-crossing movements) and that these return movements speak volumes not only of migrants' choices and experiences but also enable one to conceptualize return movements as both a circumstantial option and a process that can serve as a heuristic in better understanding the notion of home and its intersection with ethnicity and capital. I further discuss the concept of home in Chap. 7.

Returns as Heuristic

In sociological literature, a heuristic (or heuristic device) is commonly defined to be a tool for analyses; an aid that could or would give one a better interpretation or greater understanding of the social phenomenon being studied. In this section, I use the concept of return as a tool to further understand capital, home, and migration looking at the case of the Nisei.

Here, I limit the concept of return to that of a physical or corporeal return, where the return is a going back to a certain point/place/space. While not entirely fixed, this return is more often than not a concrete entity, hence a physical or a corporeal return. This is to be differentiated from a virtual return, where the experience of return is or can be mediated by information and communication technologies (ICTs) such as the internet. I also differentiate this from an "imagined return", or a return through acts of imagining and memory (Espiritu 2008: 10–11). Although I do not intend to undermine "imagined returns" but for this chapter, I limit my discussion to "actual" concrete returns.

Studies on return migration largely focus on those who returned and the society or place being returned to—usually referred to as "home" or "homeland" ("ancestral homeland" in several cases). In other cases, policies regarding return migration are looked into as well as inter-state relations and other issues tied to the return of nationals or "co-ethnics" to their "homeland". Aside from the presence of policies and laws that regulate the crossing of borders as well as encourage return migration, the process of return also has its share of several economic, socio-cultural, and political factors, not to mention the significance of social and kinship networks. Moreover, in studies of return migration, there is a need as well to look at migrants' agency and their migration process/es and experience/s, thus emphasizing not only the importance of social facts (i.e. the social fact of migration), but also the subjective meanings that the actors (migrants/returnees) have.

Return migrants in Okinawa cannot be considered to be a monolith, as they can be categorized into several groups or subgroups, and this also holds true for the Nisei. Class, social status, gender, cultural and linguistic literacy, social and kinship networks, level/s of integration, and other such categories can be used to describe these returnees.

Most literature on (ethnic) return migration to Japan focuses on the *Nikkeijin* (people of Japanese descent) who make the trip to Japan for purposes of financial stability and economic mobility. There are of course other factors that entice these people to migrate beyond the push-pull paradigm that dominates the literature. The revision of the Immigration Control and Refugee Recognition Act (ICRRA) in 1990 saw the influx of the *Nikkeijin*—most of them from Latin America—to Japan. For these *Nikkeijin*, their Japanese ancestry has served as cultural capital (Bourdieu 1926) for entry into the Japanese labour market as well as a "passport" for return migration to Japan. Being eligible for a *teijūsha* (long-term resident) visa, renewable every three years for an indefinite period of time, this set them apart from other foreign workers, and their ethnic ties to Japan make them more "favoured" by their Japanese employers (Sellek 2001: 9; de Carvalho 2003: 79; Tsuda and Cornelius 2004: 455).

As earlier mentioned, the return migration of the Nisei started in the 1970s and hence is not directly linked to the revision of the ICRRA in 1990. While the motivation for return was largely economic, there were several other reasons for the Nisei's return to their birthplace. Three main reasons are: (1) the acquisition of a Japanese nationality that translates into more (physical) mobility as well as more rights; (2) work and career stability that in turn contributes to economic and social mobility; and (3) the search for roots, that is, the Okinawan part of their ethnic identity. In short, the further accumulation of capital (i.e. economic and symbolic) as well as the emotional process/es involved in the return act itself (i.e. going back to one's birthplace, searching for one's identity) are significant in the return migration of the Nisei. To reiterate, the Nisei discussed in this book were born and raised in Okinawa and moved to the Philippines in their late childhood and adolescent years.

The return migration of the Nisei can be divided into three periods: the 1970s, the 1980s, and the 1990s to 2000s. The Nisei started returning to Okinawa as early as the 1970s. Two main macro-level factors that prompted this return are: Japan's emergence as an economic power during this period, and the political situation of the Philippines under the dictatorial Marcos regime which also sparked social insecurity and unrest. It cannot be denied that the emergence of Japan as an economic power attracted people to find work in the country and earn more than twice as much as they could in their own countries, such as the Philippines. It should also be noted that Okinawa prefecture was reverted to Japan in 1972 after being occupied by the United States since 1945, thus making Okinawa "formally" part of one of the largest economies in the world. For the Nisei, this also meant capitalizing on their part-Okinawan parentage, and the acquisition of a Japanese nationality—deemed a greater cultural capital than having a Philippine one—became more than an option for them. By cultural capital, I refer to the "symbols, ideas, tastes, and preferences that can be strategically used as resources in social action" (Scott and Marshall 2009: 148). Bourdieu (1926) states that cultural capital can also be converted into economic capital and is institutionalized (in the form of academic and educational qualifications).

The bubble years of the Japanese economy in the 1980s made Japan an attractive work destination for both for skilled and professional workers and unskilled workers. It is now common knowledge that many of these unskilled workers entered the country through various side-door and back-door mechanisms, mainly pertaining to visa status. This period was also a significant period for the return of the Nisei to Okinawa and other parts of Japan. With the Japanese economy the second largest in the world then[2] and with the economic decline of the Philippines, not a few Nisei considered going to the Japanese mainland and Okinawa to work. Their Okinawan mothers were also instrumental in encouraging the Nisei to work in Okinawa and Japan as the Philippine economy at that time did not seem to promise a better future.

Return Migration as a Circumstantial Option

Situating the Nisei within this framework, the Nisei's return migration to Okinawa is largely a return to their place of birth, whereas for those who were born and raised in the Philippines, the return is more of a return to their mother's homeland (i.e. ethnic return migration). In the case of many ethnic return migrants, including the Nisei, returns are largely linked to capital ownership as well as capital accumulation that enable these individuals to engage and participate in these kinds of migrations. Generally speaking, returns are often perceived in relation to capital accumulation, which is for the most part linked to economic capital, which in turn translates into prospects for job and financial security. This is also future-oriented as it is present-oriented, since many of the returnees desire to be assured of a better future for their own children.

It should be noted, nevertheless, that while these Nisei have been born in Okinawa and have lived there during their childhood years, the return to Okinawa was less driven by nostalgia, but rather by economic benefits of work in the prefecture. This trend is likewise seen among the Latin Americans of Japanese and Okinawan descent working in various parts of the country, where economic and financial reasons weigh more than nostalgia and/or the "search for roots". It is common knowledge that what would take years to earn in an economically less-developed country would only take a very short time to earn in an economically advanced country like Japan. Thus, the quest for a better life, and/or the prevention of "a decline in social status" (Ishi 2003: 77), particularly for those who enjoyed relatively comfortable, middle-class lives in their countries, are motivations for the return. Many Japanese-Brazilians, for instance, return migrate to Japan as a means to maintain the middle-class lives they enjoy in Brazil (Yamanaka 2000: 146). This factor may have also enticed the Nisei to embark on this journey back to the place of their birth and youth. Reaching for the "Japanese (or Okinawan) Dream"—an alternative to the "American Dream" many Filipinos long for—is not at all elusive to them as they bank on their cultural and social capital: an educated background, proficiency in English, Okinawan parentage, and social and kinship networks in the prefecture.

Nationality acquisition or naturalization also gives the migrant a much secure foothold in the host society allowing him/her to participate as a citizen. For the Nisei, nationality acquisition (*kokuseki shutoku* as opposed to naturalization or *kika*) has become one of the main reasons for return as a Japanese passport serves as capital for them as well as a means for greater (physical) mobility, which normally eludes holders of a passport from a country of the Global South, such as the Philippines. Since 2007, I have been acquainted with Daniel Itoman, a medical doctor by profession, but who works as a lecturer and researcher in several universities in Okinawa. In conversations with him whenever I visit Okinawa, Daniel told me that having either a Japanese or a Filipino citizenship "has nothing to do with your patriotism", as he considers the acquisition of citizenship in a more practical way, especially in issues of mobility. Moreover, acquiring Japanese nationality is a better option for Nisei who decide to live in Okinawa. Vincent Shimabukuro, a former base worker turned entrepreneur, gave the same reasons as Daniel since he considers having Japanese nationality as enabling easier mobility for them and is for "documentary purposes" as well. Sylvia Gomez, a former base worker who now resides in the United States with her American husband, shared the same sentiment when I met her at Oroku Catholic Church in Naha in March 2010. She also told me that she had advised a Nisei friend to apply for one since this friend of hers does not intend to go back to the Philippines. Sylvia added that the Philippine government will not be able to give support to their nationals living abroad. "They cannot support you," she said.

This acquisition of Japanese nationality also enables the Nisei to engage in both Japanese and Philippine societies in a manner characteristic of transmigrants, which are defined by Nina Glick-Schiller as "persons who, having migrated from one nation-state to another, live their lives across borders, participating simultaneously in social relations that embed them in more than one nation-state" (quoted in Waldinger 2008: 5). These transmigrants are seen to maintain "here-there connections" (Ibid). However, Alejandro Portes points out that these kinds of transmigrant activities are usually engaged in by a "distinctive immigrant minority", who are usually "educated, well-connected, and firmly established in the host country" (quoted in Waldinger 2008: 6), characteristics which the Nisei have. While holders of Japanese nationality are not allowed to have other nationalities (in contrast, the Philippines allows dual nationality), not a few of these Nisei stake a claim to Philippine nationality by resorting to several strategies to reap benefits from both nation-states, such as having businesses in both the Philippines and Okinawa, obtaining senior citizen privileges in the Philippines despite not being a resident of the country and having Japanese nationality, among others. In Chap. 4, I mentioned Noel Tōma, who told me that whenever he is in the Philippines he avails of senior citizen privileges, and said that despite being a Japanese national, he received his senior citizen card by using his Filipino name. Not quite engaging in "flexible citizenship" (Ong 1999) practices of overseas Chinese, these Nisei, with their status as Japanese nationals, are able to take advantage of political and socio-economic circumstances in both Japan and the Philippines through capital ownership and ethnic links to both countries.

Moreover, the return process is largely carried out through one's ownership of capital. I define capital ownership as an individual's own economic, cultural, and social capital that play a role/s in assisting him/her in the process of migration. These include one's ethnicity/parentage, presence of kinship and social networks in Okinawa, financial capability to make the return trip to Okinawa, membership in prefectural associations such as the Philippine Okinawan Society. The Nisei largely made the return trip to Okinawa as individual migrants (or at times accompanied by their Okinawan mothers or in some cases, they returned as a family) and were not part of any government policy (such as Philippine policies for exporting labour, changes in the Japanese Immigration Law) or labour brokerage, but are rather considered as "returning nationals", wherein cases where a Japanese passport (and thus Japanese nationality) were "automatically" granted to them either at the Japanese embassy in the Philippines or upon arrival in Okinawa, in lieu of their Philippine passport are not at all rare. Most of the Nisei I interviewed and talked to were born outside marriage. Thus, these "illegitimate" children were included in their mother's registry, providing proof of their Japanese lineage.

Nationality Acquisition of the Nisei

A large majority of the Nisei in Okinawa hold Japanese nationality, which they acquired upon their return to the prefecture. In some remarkable cases, a Japanese passport was issued to them at the Japanese embassy in Manila, before his/her departure for Japan, thus making him/her a de facto Japanese national. There are several reasons for acquiring Japanese nationality and these vary from person to person, but it is clearly due to cultural capital and increased (physical) mobility that Japanese nationality is sought over the retention of one's Philippine nationality. Residing in Japan as a Japanese national is also a much more practical option than living as a foreigner, that is with a foreign passport.

The Nisei told me how it was easy—almost "automatic"—for them to have acquired their Japanese nationality. This was because their names were listed in their Okinawan mother's family registry or *koseki*. The *koseki* system indicates pertinent details of one's family history as well as social status. It should be noted here that except for those in Miyako and the Yaeyama islands, the *koseki tōhon* (certificate of family registry) of families in the main island of Okinawa were destroyed and burned during the War. It was in 1953 that the full-scale repair of the people's *koseki* or *koseki seibi sagyō* was carried out. The whole process was completed in 1962, with the Fukuoka office handling the *koseki* of the people of Okinawa prefecture (Okuyama 2006). Most, if not all, of the cases presented here point to illegitimacy of one's birth as a factor highly likely to determine the acquisition of a Japanese nationality, as Nisei who were born out of wedlock were listed in their Okinawan mothers' *koseki*.

Japanese nationality is mainly based on membership in a *koseki*, with non-Japanese or foreigners administered separately (Wetherall 2006), thus, leaving out offspring of mixed or intercultural marriages from this system. Prior to the 1985 amendment of the Japanese Nationality Law, Japanese nationality was patrilineal and thus those with foreign fathers adopt their fathers' nationality. The Nisei were born prior to this revision and the 1950 Nationality Law recognized matrilineal acquisition of nationality for a child only in the case where the mother was unmarried (Wetherall 2006: 34). The Nisei told me how some of their siblings who were not registered in their mother's *koseki* had difficulty obtaining Japanese nationality. Hence, they could not easily acquire Japanese nationality and had to present necessary documents and undergo required processes (such as a language test) for naturalization.

The concepts of nationality and citizenship are more often than not confused and used interchangeably, despite each being very much distinct (Lee 2006: 110; Mc Crone and Kiely 2000: 19). Here, I use the concept of nationality as it is used in its Japanese form (*kokuseki*) in contrast to citizenship (*shiminken*). This reference to Japanese nationality also indicates the Nisei's legal status in Japan as well as the passport they hold. Furthermore, nationality in Japan is regarded as an "extension" of *koseki*, and thus an extension of the family (Lie 2001: 144). John Lie states the "pervasive conflation of state, nation, ethnicity, and race in contemporary Japan" where citizenship (*shiminken*) is seen as a "foreign concept" and "artificial" (Ibid). He further argues that there is a blurred distinction between "state membership and ethnonational identity"; hence nationality is considered as "natural" and a matter of fate by the Japanese (Ibid).

The Nisei's case is intriguing as circumstances surrounding their birth have led to easily access Japanese nationality. A large number of them were born out of wedlock, thus making them illegitimate offspring. These "illegitimate" ones were registered as both Filipinos and Japanese upon birth, thereby giving them an opportunity to elect either a Philippine or a Japanese nationality upon reaching the age of 21. During this time, Japanese law stipulated that children born out of wedlock to Japanese mothers were to be granted Japanese nationality. As I earlier pointed out, the 1950 Nationality Law recognized matrilineal acquisition of nationality for a child only in the case where the mother was unmarried (Wetherall 2006: 34). These "illegitimate" children were also included in their mother's *koseki*, thus providing proof of their Japanese lineage. The Japanese Nationality Law operates on the principle of *jus sanguinis* or the law of blood or descent, which in Japan specifically pertains to patrilineal descent. Anyone with a Japanese father is eligible to become a Japanese national, while those born to a Japanese mother married to a non-Japanese father are not (Murphy-Shigematsu 2000: 204). In the immediate post-war period, so-called Amerasian children born out of wedlock to Japanese women and American men became Japanese nationals, while those born to married couples became Americans as they took their father's nationality (Ibid). The Amerasian case is parallel to the case of the Nisei, where those born out of wedlock were able to acquire Japanese nationality. Those born after their parents got married are not registered in their mother's *koseki*, but are rather registered as Filipinos. In their case, they could apply for Japanese nationality with the proper documents at hand and they also need to show proof of their birth to a Japanese. Recently, a written language proficiency exam consisting of *hiragana* and *katakana* are also given to applicants.

Nisei who are non-Japanese are holders of a permanent resident visa, granted by the Ministry of Justice, which gives the holder an unlimited period of stay in Japan (Immigration Bureau, Ministry of Justice). With the 1990 amendment of the Immigration Law, the category of "long-term resident" or *teijūsha* was created, and while it is not explicitly stated in the law, this new category refers to "people of Japanese descent" or the *Nikkeijin*. For the Nisei, many of whom had returned to Okinawa (others however went to the Japanese mainland) before the revision of the law, this category does not apply hence those who do not have Japanese nationality are Filipino nationals who have permanent resident status.

While some Nisei had to apply for their Japanese nationality, which was not at all a complicated process for them as they were listed in their mother's *koseki tōhon*, some were "automatically" granted their nationality. Raphael Miyagi narrated how he was given a Japanese passport instead when he applied for a tourist visa to visit Okinawa. This was also echoed by a Nisei named Lillian Majikina, whom I met at her workplace in Kita Nakagusuku. Lillian is a primary school teacher and her students are mostly children of military base personnel. From their stories, it seems that when they first went to the Philippines after spending their childhood years in Okinawa, they were Filipino nationals; but when they went back to Okinawa, they became Japanese nationals. Lillian, who was in Okinawa for a visit (with a tourist visa) in 1990 wished to stay longer in the prefecture and so she, along with her brother, applied for a visa extension at the immigration office in Okinawa. However, the immigration officer advised them that they need not apply for a visa extension as they are Japanese nationals: "You don't have to extend your stay here because you are a Japanese citizen." Their Philippine passports then were nullified and they were given Japanese passports. Lillian told me that she was born before her parents got married; and an "illegitimate" child, under the Japanese Nationality Law before its 1985 revision, is "automatically" considered a

Japanese. Raphael was met with a similar incident when he went to the Japanese Embassy in Manila in 1971 to apply for a tourist visa to enable him to go to Okinawa, only to be given a Japanese passport. During this time, illegitimately born children (with Japanese/Okinawan mothers) "automatically" become Japanese. This was also the case of John Kohagura, another Nisei who worked on base (when I met him), who returned to Okinawa when he was 20 years old. When I met him at a Christmas party at Maehara Catholic Church in Ginowan City in December 2012, he shared how he acquired his Japanese nationality at the Japanese embassy in the Philippines. He told me that an Okinawan was working there who informed his mother about nationality acquisition. John narrated how he became an alien in the Philippines and had to pay several pesos for his Philippine visa to allow him to stay in the country. Upon his return to Okinawa, he was already a Japanese national.

Return migration points to the significant role of the state in enticing co-ethnics to enter the Japanese labour force. However, the state's role in the return movements of the Nisei, especially those that occurred between the 1970s and 1990s, seem to be insignificant and the returns were mainly carried out through one's individual (and family's) decisions (although it cannot be denied that the Okinawa prefecture's programmes for inviting overseas Okinawans and their descendants to participate in study tours and training activities also played a role in some of the Nisei's decision to return to their birthplace). In this respect, one can conceptualize return movements as a circumstantial option, which I define as an option or an alternative that migrants resort to, based on given circumstances that may be both structural (e.g. economic, political conditions) and/or personal (e.g. family matters, search for roots). Return as an option does not point to a means to an end (i.e. to gain financial security or a better livelihood), nor to a perceived end (i.e. settlement), but rather is an option that returnees take while crafting for themselves a "home" or "homes".

The whole return project should be located not only within the greater context of Japan's position in the world stage vis-à-vis the Philippines which occupies a peripheral position in relation to Japan's centre, but should also take into consideration the current role that the United States plays in the Asia-Pacific region and in world affairs. As I argued in an earlier chapter, there is a need to look at the role of U.S. hegemony and the current presence of military installations in Okinawa in the return migration of this particular group of individuals to Okinawa.

Those Who Remained

Meanwhile, to think about those who did not return or those who remained is usually the exception rather than the norm in studies of return migration. What about the non-returnees then? How can one factor in these individuals in the whole return migration process? As previously mentioned in the above discussion on return migration as a heuristic device, migration usually involves several actors and that looking at the migrant himself/herself should also take into consideration the non-migrant—the one who chose to remain, or the one who could not return. Thus, with every returnee, there is a non-returnee.

There are several reasons why the non-returnee chose to remain, or could (or would) not embark on a return movement. In the case of the Nisei, for instance, financial stability and one's career are reasons for the non-return to Okinawa. In addition, many of these Nisei cite family reasons, such as the education of their children (the *sansei*, or the third generation) in the Philippines as another factor in their decision to remain and not move to Okinawa. Moreover, while a Japanese nationality is normally considered to serve as a cultural capital, non-returnees do not view this as such and thus hold on to their Philippine nationality. This is because many of them see themselves as establishing their lives in the Philippines, with most of them living comfortable lives there. Of course, there are Nisei who desire to return but could not due to financial constraints and lack of legal necessities as opposed to their more mobile counterparts (both returnees and non-returnees).

Nevertheless, return is always an option for the non-returnees, and that decisions to return, albeit temporarily or on a short-term basis, are oftentimes made in conjunction with (familial) linkages the Nisei have in Okinawa. Many return to visit kin and friends, to study or work temporarily, to pay respects to deceased kin, to accompany their Okinawan mothers, to participate in prefectural events such as the World Uchinānchu Festival (a festival of overseas Okinawans) held every five years, among others. Hence, these two categories of returnee and non-returnee can be seen to overlap. Of course, the choice/s and opportunity/ies that the non-returnees have in the decision to return are much different from those individuals (i.e. refugees and other displaced people) who are not able to return and are forced to remain in their current place.

Return migration then should not only look at the return migrants themselves, but also take into consideration those who remained, whether by choice or not. These two categories of returnee and non-returnee are diverse in themselves, and thus intra-category comparisons are inevitable when one seeks to understand returnees and their migration processes and experiences. This same goes for non-returnees who are not a monolith, but are a diverse lot. The return is more often than not tied to a non-return, and thus, while comparisons are evident in this regard, this linkage is also crucial in understanding transnational migration and what the mere act of crossing (nation-state) borders says about inter-state relations.

Notes

1. Here, I define adult as a person of legal age (the age when one is considered an adult) in the Philippine context, that is 18 years old. This is because the return movement occurred from the Philippines back to Okinawa. It should be noted though that in Japan the legal age is 20 years old.
2. From 1968–2010, before it was overtaken by China, Japan was the largest economy, next only to the United States of America. (See https://asialinkbusiness.com.au/japan/getting-started-in-japan/japans-economy?doNothing=1)

References

Bourdieu, P. (1926). The Forms of Capital. In J. Richardson (Ed.), *Handbook of Theory of Research for the Sociology of Education* (pp. 46–58). New York: Greenwood Press.

Cassarino, J. P. (2004). Theorising Return Migration: The Conceptual Approach to Return Migrants Revisited. *International Journal on Multicultural Societies, 6*(2), 253–279.

de Carvalho, D. (2003). *Migrants and Identity in Japan and Brazil: The Nikkeijin*. London: Routledge.

Espiritu, Y. L. (2008). *Homebound: Filipino American Lives Across Cultures, Communities, and Countries* (Philippine edition). Quezon City: Ateneo de Manila University Press.

Ishi, A. (2003). Searching for Home, Wealth, Pride, and "Class": Japanese Brazilians in the "Land of Yen". In J. Lesser (Ed.), *Searching for Home Abroad: Japanese Brazilians and Transnationalism*. Durham: Duke University Press.

Japan's Economy. *Asia Link Business*. https://asialinkbusiness.com.au/japan/geting-started-in-japan/japans-economy?doNothing=1. Accessed 14 June 2019.

Lee, S. (2006). The Cultural Exclusiveness of Ethnocentrism: Japan's treatment of Foreign Residents. In S. Lee, S. Murphy-Shigematsu, & H. Befu (Eds.), *Japan's Diversity Dilemmas: Ethnicity, Citizenship, and Education* (pp. 100–124). Lincoln: iUniverse, Inc.

Lie, J. (2001). *Multi-ethnic Japan*. Cambridge: Harvard University Press.
Long, L. D., & Oxfeld, E. (Eds.). (2004). *Coming Home? Refugees, Migrants, and Those Who Stayed Behind*. Philadelphia: University of Pennsylvania Press.
Mc Crone, D., & Kiely, R. (2000). Nationalism and Citizenship. *Sociology*, *34*(1), 19–34.
Murphy-Shigematsu, S. (2000). Identities of Multiethnic People in Japan. In M. Douglass & G. Roberts (Eds.), *Japan and Global Migration: Foreign Workers and the Advent of a Multicultural Society* (pp. 198–218). London: Routledge.
Okuyama, K. (2006). Sengo Okinawa no Hōtaisei to Koseki no Hensen. *Yokohama Kokusai Shakaikagaku Kenkyū*, *11*(3), 349–368.
Ong, A. (1999). *Flexible Citizenship: The Cultural Logics of Transnationality*. Durham: Duke University Press.
Piore, M. J. (1979). *Birds of Passage: Migrant Labor and Industrial Societies*. Cambridge: Cambridge University Press.
Scott, J., & Marshall, G. (Eds.). (2009). *Oxford Dictionary of Sociology* (3rd ed.). Oxford: Oxford University Press.
Sellek, Y. (2001). *Migrant Labour in Japan*. Hampshire: Palgrave.
Tsuda, T. (Ed.). (2009). *Disaporic Homecomings: Ethnic Return Migration in Comparative Perspective*. Stanford: Stanford University Press.
Tsuda, T., & Cornelius, W. A. (2004). Japan: Government Policy, Immigrant Reality. In W. A. Cornelius, T. Tsuda, P. L. Martin, & J. E. Hollifield (Eds.), *Controlling Immigration: A Global Perspective* (2nd ed., pp. 439–476). Stanford: Stanford University Press.
Waldinger, R. (2008). Between "Here" and "There": Immigrant Cross-Border Activities and Loyalties. *International Migration Review*, *42*(1), 3–29.
Wetherall, W. (2006). Nationality in Japan. In S. Lee, S. Murphy-Shigematsu, & H. Befu (Eds.), *Japan's Diversity Dilemmas: Ethnicity, Citizenship, and Education* (pp. 11–46). Lincoln: iUniverse, Inc.
Xiang, B. (2014). The Return of Return: Migration, Asia, and Theory. In G. Batistella (Ed.), *Global and Asian Perspectives in International Migration* (pp. 167–182). Cham: Springer International Publishing.
Yamanaka, K. (2000). "I Will Go Home, But When?" Labor Migration and Circular Diaspora Formation by Japanese Brazilians in Japan. In M. Douglass & G. S. Roberts (Eds.), *Japan and Global Migration: Foreign Workers and the Advent of a Multicultural Society*. London: Routledge.

CHAPTER 6

The Other Army: United States Forces in Japan Employees in Okinawa

> *To choose a life of dedication to one's country is a hard choice. To sacrifice comfort to work in an environment that is culturally different can be a hard choice. To be an USFJ employee, is to be a bridge between nations, a link in the chain that binds our countries' futures together.*
> Message from USFJ, USFJ Employment Guide: 3

Okinawa, with its large number of military bases, has a high proportion of civilians working inside these facilities. To accomplish the mission that the United States Forces in Japan (USFJ) have been tasked to do, civilian employees, known as USFJ employees, are being employed by the Japanese government to work on these military installations. USFJ employees "are employees who are hired by the Government of Japan (through the Minister of Defence) for the purpose of accomplishing the mission of the United States Forces in Japan and work on the USFJ facilities" (LMO/IAA website). These USFJ employees are mainly employed through the Labour Management Organization for USFJ Employees, Incorporated Administrative Agency (LMO/IAA), an agency separate from, but working closely with the Ministry of Defence of the Government of Japan. The agency is said to provide "high-quality services to the USFJ employees in order to secure the workforce for the U.S. forces stationed in Japan in accordance with the Japan-U.S. Security Treaty" (LMO/IAA website). There are around 26,000 USFJ employees working throughout Japan to "support the activities of the USFJ", and these employees work in a wide

© The Author(s) 2020
J. O. Zulueta, *Transnational Identities on Okinawa's Military Bases*,
https://doi.org/10.1007/978-981-32-9787-6_6

87

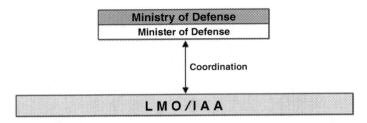

Fig. 6.1 Relationship between the Ministry of Defence and the LMO/IAA. (Source: http://www.lmo.go.jp/english/purpose/index.html)

range of positions such as clerks, technicians, security guards, waiters/waitresses, cooks, and sales clerks, among others—positions deemed necessary to operate these military facilities. The hiring of these base workers is carried out by the Labour Management Office, Incorporated Administrative Agency (LMO/IAA). This agency also handles other administrative matters such as recruitment, labour management, wage, health, and welfare (Ibid). Previously, however, the hiring of USFJ employees was under the jurisdiction of each prefectural government before it relinquished its duty to the LMO/IAA in April 2002. Figure 6.1 illustrates the relationship between the Ministry of Defence and the LMO/IAA.

As stated in the LMO/IAA webpage as well as in the USFJ Employment Guide, USFJ employees, although employed by the Ministry of Defence, are not considered as government employees. However, it is the Government of Japan, through the Ministry of Defence, that oversees the work contracts and salaries of the employees in coordination with the LMO/IAA. On the other hand, work supervision, training, and other guidance are under the jurisdiction of the U.S. government through the USFJ. This is all possible under the banner of the U.S.-Japan Security Treaty (Fig. 6.2).

Civilians who work on these military installations are involved in a variety of jobs from semi-skilled to highly skilled, and are engaged in various types of work. There are three types of labour contracts available for USFJ employees: (1) Master Labour Contract (MLC); (2) Mariner's Contract (MC); and (3) Indirect Hire Agreement (IHA). The MLC is related to work on the headquarters or units of the commands, while the MC is for jobs related to those who work on the non-combatant ship. Meanwhile, the IHA is an agreement that concerns those who work in mess halls and exchanges (shops, services) in the USFJ facilities (LMO website). In all three of these

6 THE OTHER ARMY: UNITED STATES FORCES IN JAPAN EMPLOYEES... 89

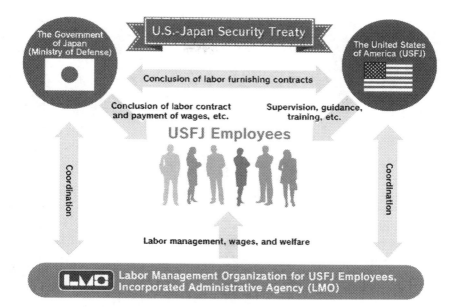

Fig. 6.2 Status of USFJ employees. (Source: USFJ Employment Guide 2018, page 4: https://www.lmo.go.jp/recruitment/pdf/pamphlet_en.pdf)

labour contracts, work is mostly on U.S. military bases for the provision of support services. According to the USFJ Employment Guide, employees are "required to have special skills and English language abilities" depending on the type of job (USFJ Employment Guide 2018: 14). For jobs that fall under the MLC and MC, members of the USFJ and its civilian components and dependents are not eligible to be hired for these jobs. Meanwhile, U.S. civilian personnel (i.e. those who hold U.S. nationality) cannot be hired for jobs that fall under the IHA (Ibid). Most of my Nisei informants as well as people who I met and talked to in the course of my research were either on MLC or IHA contracts. The Marine Corps Community Services (MCCS), Army and Air Force Exchange Service (AAFES), and the Aerospace Medical Squadron (AMDS/SGPM) are some of the units where these second-generation base workers are affiliated with.

Based on a ten-year employment data I culled from the years 2008 to 2017,[1] an average of 3402 people have been hired as USFJ employees every year. From 2013 to 2017, there was a steady increase of individuals hired for work on base. Meanwhile, the average number of retirees per

Table 6.1 Number of USFJ employees and retirees (ten-year overview, 2008–2017)

	2008	2009	2010	2011	2012	2013	2014	2015	2016	2017
Hired employees	3234	3460	3201	2943	3077	3042	3289	3711	3875	4192
Retired employees	3009	3117	3165	3255	3264	3141	3348	3599	3708	3889

Source: LMO/IIA website, http://www.lmo.go.jp/results/index.html

year is at 3349 in this ten-year span, with the years 2014–2017 showing a steady increase in the number of retired individuals. Table 6.1 below gives more detailed information on this.

It was mentioned that the number of USFJ employees has been increasing and that it was found to be positively correlated with the amount of host nation support (HNS) that Japan provides for the U.S. base presence (Yoda 2006: 951) as stipulated in the U.S.-Japan Treaty. Through statistical data, Yoda argues that the increase in the HNS also contributed to the increase in the number of local (Japanese) base workers relative to U.S. military personnel. In the ten-year data I provided above, while there were some fluctuations, it can also be observed that the number of USFJ employees generally increased in this ten-year span despite a drop in the number of hired workers in 2011. The numbers picked up again from 2014.

Most of the USFJ employees are stationed in Okinawa, with around 9002 USFJ employees working on bases by the end of November 2017. The only prefecture that has a little more USFJ employees than Okinawa is Kanagawa prefecture, which hosts the Yokosuka Naval Base and the Naval Air Facility Atsugi, with 9155 employees as of November 2017 (USFJ Employment Guide 2018: 18). While most USFJ employees are Japanese nationals, the Employment Guide states that "no specific nationality" is said to be required, as long as one is not a national of the United States (including individuals with dual nationality) (see USFJ Employment Guide 2018: 16). For non-Japanese nationals, a work permit is needed.

USFJ Employees in Okinawa

For people who live their lives surrounded by these military facilities, the experience of living in a place where military aircraft flying overhead are frequent sensory encounters, in addition to seeing and meeting American soldiers and base personnel visiting restaurants, bars, and other establishments outside the bases, have been part of the everyday lives of these people. Base work also becomes an attractive employment option for many of the locals, and there is no doubt that the presence of these bases has its economic benefits for the residents of these base towns and nearby areas. It was said that base work has more "freedom" and benefits as compared to local Japanese companies, and local government units in the prefecture are known to encourage its constituents to work on these U.S. bases. A quick search on several of these Okinawan cities' and towns' websites revealed information posted about recruitment for USFJ employees.

A case in point is Kin Town, a base town centrally located on the main island of Okinawa, where Camp Hansen, a Marine Corps Base, is located. According to the town's official website, an information session for USFJ jobs was held last 13 December 2018 at the central community centre (*chuō kōminkan*). The town government pointed out that some facilities from Camp Kinser and Camp Zukeran (Camp Foster)—both Marine Corps Bases—will be transferred to Camp Hansen in Kin Town, and for this, there will be a need to recruit new USFJ employees. The page also indicates that there is a move from the town government to give locals priority in hiring, thus the reason for organizing the explanatory session (Kin Town Official Website: https://www.town.kin.okinawa.jp/topics/detail/4840). Moreover, a quick search on the website of Hello Work (the Japanese government's Employment Service Centre that provides information on job recruitment and placement) also shows the availability of jobs on base, mostly through IHA contracts, where local Japanese companies are contracted to provide services within these military installations. This just goes to show that work on base is a lucrative source of livelihood for many Okinawans, particularly those living in proximity to these U.S. bases.

The LMO actively recruits workers on base for a variety of jobs, mostly on MLC and IHA contracts. The LMO also boasts of a work-life balance for its employees as well as seriously takes on its goal to have more female representation in the workplace, where roughly around one-fourth (26 per cent) of USFJ employees are women (data as of April 2017, USFJ Employment Guide 2018: 11). The Employment Guide also features several interviews with USFJ employees—both men and women—about working for the USFJ. Most of those featured spoke about the opportunities to hone their abilities—especially English language skills—at work, maintaining a work-life balance, having the chance to contribute to the betterment of their community, experiencing American culture and interacting with American colleagues, among other things. Base work then, is painted as a satisfying career that everyone can engage in.

While for the most part base employees are mostly Japanese nationals, a significant percentage of these USFJ employees in Okinawa are of both Okinawan and Filipino parentage, who are identified here as Nisei. As mentioned in Chap. 5, these Nisei acquired Japanese nationality upon their return to Okinawa, and a large number of them have secured base-related jobs. Base work is considered lucrative for these individuals as opposed to work outside the bases that demand proficiency in Japanese, as without the necessary language skills, these individuals are relegated to low-skilled work, much like their *Nikkeijin* counterparts, such as the Japanese-Brazilians in the Japanese mainland, who are mostly engaged in low-skilled work in factories. For the Nisei in Okinawa, base work has been an opportunity for them to be more socially mobile; and base work is easily available to them due to their educational background and high proficiency in the English language. This was also acknowledged by the Nisei themselves, with not a few of them saying that they have an edge over the locals (as well as the mainland Japanese) as they have higher English proficiency levels. English proficiency is one thing, but what needs to be noted here is the ability of Filipinos to adapt to and acquire an American (or a near-American) accent, which can be traced to large-scale American influence in terms of education, popular culture, and the media. I noticed that most of the Nisei I spoke to, specifically those who work on base, speak with a slight American accent, probably because of the need to adapt to the Americans' speech patterns and pronunciation. I should also add here Filipinos' affinity with American culture due to an almost 50-year-long colonial history. For the Nisei themselves, work on base gives them opportunities to improve on whatever skills they have, as work outside the bases, particularly work in Japanese companies or industries, require a significant degree of Japanese language proficiency. Thus, those having insufficient Japanese language abilities might have difficulty in obtaining work outside, or will be relegated to low-skilled work.

Meanwhile, based on my interviews with the Nisei who work on base, it was made known to me that some civilian employees of these U.S. military installations get paid higher than other government employees, since base workers even receive bonuses and other benefits such as an "English language allowance". This so-called Language Allowance Degree (LAD) entitles one to a language allowance for as long as he or she takes an English language exam and qualify for one of the four LAD levels, the lowest of which is Level 1. Those who manage to attain the third and fourth levels are qualified for higher positions on base. This was shared to me by Sonny Uechi, a former base worker (now retired), back in March 2010. Regarding the LAD, Sonny told me that one could opt not to take the exam, but he/she will not be eligible to receive the allowance. A language allowance, along with a differential allowance, was included in base employees' salaries (Yoda 2006: 940). However, it seems that these allowances have been abolished by the Ministry of Defence, based on a 2008 document informing USFJ employees based in the North Kanto area of the plan to scrap this category (https://www.mod.go.jp/rdb/n-kanto/oshirase/lmd-notification.pdf). A look at the USFJ Employment Guide would also confirm that a language allowance is not anymore part of the major allowances listed on the guide (USFJ Employment Guide: 15).

Meanwhile, Vincent Shimabukuro, a former base worker who was employed as an engineer in a construction company on base through the IHA, told me that base work is lucrative employment due to the benefits the employees receive. He estimated that around 70 to 80 per cent of the Nisei in Okinawa work on base. Even his twin brothers both work on base, he told me when I first met him in 2007. Vincent said that base workers hired by the Japanese government enjoy more benefits than their counterparts hired by the U.S. government (such as American citizens, Filipino-Americans) as they also receive two bonuses (summer and winter bonuses) a year. Moreover, he thinks that educational attainment is not of absolute importance when applying for jobs on base, as long as one has the needed English skills to do base work. He mentioned that his brothers who only received an undergraduate education in the Philippines were hired to work on base and—at the time of my interview—are currently holding good positions. "Attaining this degree or [that] is a plus of course, but communicating in English is a bigger plus for them," Vincent added. He said that there were even cases where Filipino Navy personnel (who are already naturalized Americans) would tease the Nisei: "How come I have a higher rank than you, but you still get higher pay than me?" He added that the Nisei working on base are really hard workers, compared to their local counterparts who occupy much lower positions because of their insufficient English language skills. Vincent also added that one could work on base even if he or she does not possess a Japanese licence (e.g. engineering licence), as long as one has received a proper degree needed in the job. Based on his own experience, he said that engineering graduates from the Philippines are recognized for work on base even if they do not possess a Japanese engineering licence.

As I previously stated, base work is being portrayed as a gratifying experience for USFJ employees. For the Nisei, work on these U.S. military installations also seemed to be fulfilling for many of them especially when they spoke of their relationships with their colleagues, such as how they enjoyed working with multicultural colleagues—Japanese, Americans, Filipinos, and other nationalities—on base. They spoke of how people were friendly and open. When she was working as a manager at a fast-food restaurant on base, Stephanie Ojana—whom I introduced in Chap. 1—spoke of how she was able to establish close relationships with her workmates, including Americans, who gained her trust and trusted her as well. She even told me that her American friends used to ask her to teach them Japanese or to translate for them, as they knew that she was part-Okinawan. She laughingly told me then in Filipino, "*Ako pa ang mag-tuturo sa inyo, e baluktot nga yung Japanese ko eh* (with my broken Japanese, should I be the one to teach you)?" With what she shared, Stephanie managed to portray a friendly and relaxed environment when she talked about her work. On a sunny December day in 2012, I was with Bobby Katsukata, a Nisei, at Camp Foster to have lunch with Enrico Jamora (whom I talked about in Chap. 3) at the Ocean Breeze Restaurant. Before meeting with Enrico, Bobby took me on a short tour of the Camp, where I met his American colleagues. He turned to me and said, "this is how they are", pointing to the friendly disposition of his workmates and how he said it is easy to get along with his American colleagues. Indeed, one can conclude that work on base for both locals and the Nisei is an endeavour that is appealing for its work environment and the opportunities it presents for skills training and development, particularly for one's English language proficiency.

To reiterate, USFJ employees support the United States Forces in Japan and work for the functioning and maintenance of U.S. military installations in the country. It should be noted, however, that support for the U.S. military and their dependents does not end with base work, since off-base employment in affiliated industries also plays a role in making these people's lives in Okinawa (and in other base towns as well) comfortable. I refer to them in the next section.

Off-Base Work in Okinawa

In connection to the so-called missions of overseas U.S. bases to provide work and income for the military-industrial complex and to ensure that the military and their families live comfortably while serving abroad (Johnson 2004: 152), the roles that off-base employees play in this regard should not be overlooked. One of the conditions that enable and sustain the presence of military bases in the world is the demand for people to address the needs of the U.S. military and their families—even outside of these so-called military "enclaves". These include teachers, sales clerks, and service staff such as waiters/waitresses, and cooks. Musicians and other entertainers are also sought to entertain military personnel in these overseas bases. Furthermore, there are the numerous bars and pubs that encircle these military bases that once employed local women and up until recent years began to hire workers from overseas, particularly from the Philippines.

There are also off-base establishments that cater to the U.S. military and their families, many of which are local businesses, such as bars/pubs, restaurants, and tailors. A significant off-base facility that is worth mentioning here is the Seamen's Club. The Seamen's Club, a restaurant and entertainment facility located next to the Naha Military Port in Naha City, is said to be an organization that provides assistance to seafarers and shares a no-tax "preferential status" as the U.S. military facilities (Funabashi 1999: 139). The Seamen's Club is not restricted to Americans—there are Japanese members as well—as membership is open for a fee of 5000 yen per year, entitling one to dine in the restaurant.[2] A bar, which only opens at night, as well as a souvenir shop (which sells PX goods), is also housed in the building. Since the location of the Seamen's Club is in a civilian area, former Okinawa governor, Ota Masahide, campaigned for the facility to be relocated inside a U.S. base (Ibid). A large number of the staff who works in the restaurant is Nisei. During my visit there in March 2010, I became acquainted with Rie Ong, also a Nisei, who was working as a waitress in the restaurant. She has been living in Okinawa for 20 years when I met her. Another Nisei, Namiko Higa, was also working as a waitress at the Seamen's Club. In our short conversations, they told me that Americans favoured Filipinos and Nisei like them as they are conversant in English and can generally get along well with Americans.

I also would like to note that there are Nisei who work as pre-school teachers, with some of them owning their own pre-schools. There are of course Filipino nationals who work as pre-school teachers in their own schools; these people are married to an Okinawan or a mainland Japanese, or to a Nisei. Among the Nisei who work as pre-school teachers in Okinawa is Lillian Majikina, who at the same time co-owns the school—Sakura Preschool—where she was teaching. I got acquainted with Lillian in March 2010 and visited her school while classes were ongoing. Most of her students are children of American base personnel, and she said that a lot of these Americans entrust their children's primary schooling to these off-base schools owned and managed by Filipinos (non-Nisei) and Nisei. It can be said that the presence of the U.S. military and their families in Okinawa helps in sustaining the education businesses of these Nisei as there is still demand for off-base primary school education in English despite the presence of on-base schools, which are less expensive for base personnel.

Lillian mentioned that most of the international schools outside the bases cater to children of the U.S. military and personnel. There are of course pre-schools inside these bases but many American parents prefer to send their children to these off-base schools for their pre-school education. When I asked her why, Lillian shared that those schools managed and owned by the Nisei (and the Filipinos), focus on the academic development of children and students are taught basic reading and writing skills at a much earlier age. This kind of education is patterned after a more Asian, or as Lillian said, a Philippine-style education, which gives more emphasis to a child's academic development. This is in contrast to schools on base, where much more focus is given to children's development through crafts and play. She added that U.S. pre-schools, on the other hand, emphasize the socialization of children. However, in 2009, pre-schools on base shifted their teaching emphasis and began to adopt more academic ways of teaching. This change was attributed to the fact that base personnel, particularly those parents who are academically conscious, prefer to send their children to study in schools outside the base, and hence schools on base have to contend with these off-base Nisei (and Filipino)-owned schools. These "new" pre-schools on base also offer free education, prompting enrolment levels in her school to go down. Lillian also shared that elementary schools on base usually do not charge tuition fees, but pre-schools do, and these fees are computed according to the military personnel's rank. With the change in the pre-school system inside the bases, as well as the free tuition these offer, the future of off-base schools seems uncertain.

This chapter gave an overview of civilian base work in Japan as well as the underlying mechanisms and organization involved in the hiring and employment of these so-called United States Forces in Japan employees. These employees play a significant role in the maintenance and the day-to-day workings of these military installations. What is more poignant in this regard, is the absence or the seeming absence of discrimination and prejudice experienced by these USFJ employees—Nisei included—in contrast to the TCNs employed by the United States Occupation Government during the immediate post-war years. This may be due to the cultural capital that the Nisei have that enabled them to acquire favourable jobs on base. In addition, their familiarity with American customs enables them to easily adjust to base work culture. What is ironic though is that for many of these Nisei, experiences of discrimination were to be found outside their workplaces, that is, in everyday Okinawan society. For the Nisei, Okinawa is their natal home; but the question of where home is, still remains a question for many of them. I examine this issue further in the next chapter.

Notes

1. Current data (as of February 2019) posted on the LMO website only include numbers for the years 2015 to 2017. Data from 2008 to 2010 were posted on the website when I was writing my dissertation in 2010, and data from 2011 to 2014 were available when I presented a related paper at a conference in March 2016.
2. This information was provided by the Nisei I met at the Club when I had lunch with a Filipino I met while on fieldwork at Oroku Church in 2010.

References

Funabashi, Y. (1999). *Alliance Adrift*. New York: Council on Foreign Relations Press.
Johnson, C. (2004). *The Sorrows of Empire: Militarism, Secrecy, and the End of the Republic*. London: Verso.
Labour Management Organization for USFJ Employees, Incorporated Administrative Agency (LMO/IAA) website: http://www.lmo.go.jp
Notification to USFJ Employees, Ministry of Defence: https://www.mod.go.jp/rdb/n-kanto/oshirase/lmd-notification.pdf. Accessed 3 May 2019.
Official Webpage of Kin Town: https://www.town.kin.okinawa.jp/topics/detail/4840. Accessed 3 May 2019.
United States Forces in Japan (USFJ) Employment Guide 2018: https://www.lmo.go.jp/recruitment/pdf/pamphlet_en.pdf. Accessed 7 February 2019.
Yoda, T. (2006). Japan's Host Nation Support Program for the U.S.-Japan Security Alliance: Past and Prospects. *Asian Survey, 46*(6), 937–961.

CHAPTER 7

"Home Is where the Heart Is?" An Invisible Minority

THE QUESTION OF HOME

What and where is home for the Nisei? What and who defines a home?

The notion of home is ubiquitous. In the fashioning of a sense of place in society (or in the world), almost everyone talks about or points to a home, and this includes not only migrants or people who move, but also people who do not move, that is, those who remain. Doreen Massey has this to say:

It is interesting to note how frequently the characterization of place as home comes from those who have left, and it would be fascinating to explore how often this characterization is framed around those who—perforce—stayed behind. (Massey 1994: 166)

For people who remain, those who "do not move", it would be apparent that their perceptions of home would be influenced by their everyday experiences of "not moving". Home would probably be a fixed entity for them and will not be subject to processes of creating and re-creating, much less be something to be yearned for and be nostalgic about. Oftentimes, home is taken for granted, as it is a product of the everyday, so much so that the "going home" or the "coming home" has become routinized and devoid of any meaning. On the other hand, for people who move, home would take on a different meaning as they fashion out a sense of place in the process of their migrations/movements, and here I include return migrations.

"Home" as "Place"; "Home" as "Consciousness"

For the Nisei, home may refer to a particular place, such as the concrete structure of a house/home, that is a place of residence, in its literal sense. Home may also refer to the family—that which makes a house a home, where house would essentially point to the structure itself, while home would indicate the presence of interrelationships in this structure or place of dwelling. Yet, for some, home may mean the presence of a community and one's belongingness to that particular community—be it a small community of churchgoers, or the larger community of an ethnic group residing in a certain country. Taking off from this point, the notion of home may point to the nation or a nation-state, such that a nation can stand in for a person's home (for instance, a migrant "dislocated" for a long time from his/her place of birth, may "feel at home" in another country, but feel alienated in his/her natal country despite the presence of kin and friends there, etc.). However, the relationship of home to belongingness and to "feeling at home" is also tied to notions of identity and one's perception of the Self vis-à-vis the Other. Hence, home is also "something that is sought, imagined, and recreated" (Abdelhady 2008: 63). It is a conscious creation and recreation of the subject (i.e. migrant or "return" migrant) as he/she is engaged in the transitory process of return.

Home, then, as the "creation and imagination of consciousness (*ishiki no sōzō to sōzō*)" (Iyotani 2007: 5), I argue, continues to change under conditions of globality. Along with this, one's sense of a home, which differs across migrant generations, entails the question of one's identity and also continues to be transformed. In a continuously mobile world within which people physically migrate and move from border to border, the notion of one's home is influenced by formations of one's identity, and as identities are always in flux and are malleable, perceptions of home also change along with it. Border-crossings and migrations contribute to changes in one's consciousness of a home as the point of origin and/or the place of destination may or may not be home, that is, home may be either one place or both places at the same time, or nowhere at all. The migrant, as a conscious subject, imagines and constructs what and where his/her home is.

Meanwhile, the concept of home has both spatial and temporal dimensions. The place of one's birth is a poor indicator of homeland or home especially if migration from that place happened at an early stage in a person's life (Newbold 2001: 23–24). Likewise, the place of migration may turn out to be home for the migrant especially if he or she has lived there for more than half of his or her life. The birthplace then would just be a distant memory, a place alien to the migrant, and the current society being lived in, the more familiar one. With regards to this, it should be remembered that these Nisei moved to the Philippines at an early age. Besides this, their exposure to aspects of Okinawan culture was limited as their mothers concealed their Okinawan identities in a conscious attempt at assimilation to avoid discrimination from the locals (who considered the Okinawans to be Japanese), whose memories of the Second World War were still vividly etched in their minds. Hence it can be argued that whatever memory these Nisei have of the Okinawa of their childhood are but distant memories; and their small amount (or lack thereof) of exposure to Okinawan language and culture, as well as their constant exposure to Philippine culture and norms during their stay in the Philippines, may have shaped their conceptions of where and what their home is. It should also be mentioned here that the post-war atmosphere in the Philippines was not at all pleasant for the Nisei as well since most of them experienced discrimination from their peers for being half-Okinawan.[1] Experiences of discrimination when they were young may have also shaped their identity and belongingness, which are seen as significant factors in the question of home. Their part-Okinawan and part-Filipino parentage nonetheless influenced their conceptions of home as well as the purposes of their return. In this regard, home is inextricably tied to notions of return, wherein the latter is continually being formed and recreated by the former, and vice versa.

"Home as consciousness" posits the subject as an active agent in the process of "home-making" and the creation of his/her home. Notions of home (and return) are contingent on social processes, and the social construction of home also adapts to cultural, economic, political, and social changes, such that home (much like the concept of return) is not a fixed entity, and is dependent on the migrant's experiences and perceptions of the everyday.

Moreover, social constructions of home, place, and belonging are not only dependent on ethnicity and one's ties to a so-called ethnic homeland since they are also "conditional upon a legal and social status as well as upon the economic and political relations in the new country and its imperial legacy" (Moreton-Robinson 2003: 29). For the Nisei, who mostly occupy middle-class status in Okinawa and are Japanese nationals, calling Okinawa home may either mean a temporary or a permanent place for them to settle in, while to other people of Okinawan ethnicity or the *Nikkeijin*, who mostly work unskilled jobs and do not enjoy the benefits of a Japanese nationality, Okinawa may not be even seen as home and is probably just considered a place to earn and save enough money to bring back to their countries. Furthermore, the Nisei in Okinawa can be said to occupy a different position from other migrants (i.e. the *Nikkeijin*, Latin Americans of Okinawan descent, Taiwanese, Filipinos, etc.) and hence their conceptions of home, place, and belonging are produced and experienced differently.

Narrating Home

> Migrancy...involves a movement in which neither the points of departure nor those of arrival are immutable or certain...Always in transit, the promise of a homecoming...becomes an impossibility. (Iain Chambers 1994: 5)

In this section, I look at how the Nisei define what and where home is. Their birth in Okinawa, their migration to the Philippines, and eventual return to Okinawa—although transitory, and is defined by their transmigratory character—I argue, are significant events in their lives that influenced their perceptions of home. Their "narrations of home"—talking of home and return—as well, argues against the common assumption of a single home, as they speak of having several homes.

The stories of the Nisei who returned to Okinawa speak very much of homes as they do of returns. The notion of home is always tied to a going back or return, and thus to conceive home away from motion (return), is to extinguish the very essence of the word. Nevertheless, a return can also be perceived of as returns, in that the return may not solely (or may not even) point to a point of origin, but to a point of destination. Some Nisei spoke of returning as both a return to Okinawa and a return to the Philippines, such that the return may be here or there. In this regard, is the transitory nature of return also seen as negating the notion of a home and hence denying a homecoming? As Iain Chambers notes, can we consider a homecoming, then, as an "impossibility"? Does the transitory nature of the return yield nothing but a distant memory of home, in that the perceived home of the returnee (i.e. home as Okinawa and/or the Philippines) is in actuality a mirage—one that reflects the expectations (of home) of the migrant, which is tied to perceptions about himself/herself (i.e. one's identity)?

While there are no clear answers to the questions I raised above, homecoming for the returnee may yield unfavourable experiences to the returnee himself/herself, especially when expectations of a welcome from what was/is perceived to be home may be in contradiction with reality. It is apparent that temporal factors are very much involved here as communities and societies are far from stagnant as they change over time. Also, for many of these return migrants, spending several years in another country had influenced their behaviours, thoughts, and practically most aspects of their lives, such that their home might not "feel like home" to them; and for the people that remained, these returnees become more like "strangers in the (ethnic) homeland" (Tsuda 2003), and not the people who once were part of their daily lives.

Unfamiliarity with the "new" environment upon the return home would probably present problems for the returnee particularly if he/she only has vague memories of his/her stay there, due to migration at an early age. This is usually the case of the Nisei who left Okinawa for the Philippines at an early age, some even younger than five years old. Culture shock, failure to adjust due to unfamiliarity with the customs and language, might cause disillusionment in many of these returnees. Sylvia Gomez, who returned to Okinawa when she was in her 20s and managed to acquire Japanese nationality making her (legally) "Japanese", told me that she was not really happy with her life in Okinawa then. She felt that she was "handicapped":

> Half of my senses are handicapped, I don't see, I can only see half, I don't see everything because I cannot read. You cannot speak it (the Japanese language), you cannot express yourself, or you cannot hear everything, because even though you hear it, you don't understand, so I feel like I'm really half, half-handicapped, *iyon ang feeling ko talaga* (that's what I really feel).

To be "handicapped" due to one's insufficient language ability (considering the fact that the Nisei are ethnically part-Okinawan) implies not being able to function as a "complete" and efficient member of the society that is supposedly, or should be (one's) home. It points to a "dysfunction" on the part of the returnee as he or she is not able to function as a (full) member of his or her community/society. Likewise, it also indicates "dislocations"—which "define the experience of migration from the perspective of the migrant subject" (Parreñas 2003: 31)—in that the place once lived in, turns distant and becomes a whole new different place, as he/she becomes a "stranger" to and in it. Home then becomes an unfamiliar place.

Raphael Miyagi likewise experienced this language "handicap" upon returning to Okinawa. On his first day of work at Camp Kinser in 1972, he talked about getting on the wrong bus and being unable to explain himself clearly to the driver as his Japanese was not yet sufficient to allow him to communicate well. The driver eventually told him that he rode on the wrong bus and gave him instructions to get to Camp Kinser. He also merrily shared an incident where he made mistakes in filling out a medical questionnaire, and accidentally replied "yes" to the question: "*Ninshin shite imasu ka*", which means, "Are you pregnant?", prompting the nurse to call him and say, "*Miyagi-san, Miyagi-san, ninshin shiteirun desu ka? Dansei deshou?* (Miyagi-san, Miyagi-san, are you pregnant? You're a male, right?)" Raphael laughed at the thought of several embarrassments he experienced due to his insufficient Japanese ability. Nevertheless, he believes that there is no room for self-pity and that one must do something when faced with this kind of situation. He then decided to study the language on his own.

While Lillian Majikina's initial return to Okinawa in 1990 to visit her relatives very much translated to a welcome home for her and her brother, since money was sent to them for their trip and their mother's family provided for their board and lodging for three months, Lillian said that she experienced culture shock as she was not accustomed to the cultural and social codes in her mother's family and in Okinawa. This could be expected as Lillian herself migrated to the Philippines when she was only five years old, and due to her mother's early death, she was brought up by her aunt in the Philippines. Hence it could be said that Lillian was brought up in a more Filipino way as compared to other Nisei who were personally brought up by their Okinawan mothers. This, as well as the years Lillian spent living in the Philippines before returning to Okinawa contributed to her feelings of "dislocation" in her natal homeland.

For many returnees, one's ethnic homeland or natal homeland does not become home due to the "lost familiarity" of what was once considered home. For the Nisei, many of whom left Okinawa for the Philippines in their childhood, the familiar is but a distant memory, and what greets them upon their return to Okinawa is a largely unfamiliar setting and a vastly different culture. While the Nisei have surpassed these hurdles and have managed to integrate themselves in Okinawan culture and society, Okinawa as home at times contradicts reality, as the return home, more often than not, is greeted with a cold shoulder—family and kin in Okinawa treat the Nisei differently as if they were strangers and not family. As an illustration of this, I take up Sylvia's case. Sylvia said that when her mother returned to Okinawa, she experienced discrimination due to the fact that she married a foreigner. She also said that despite the presence of her Okinawan relatives in Okinawa, she and her husband always stay at a hotel on their visits, as they were not even invited to stay and/or visit their relatives' homes. She added that her relatives treat her differently since they consider her to be a Filipino. Moreover, she laments that even her mother's own family treated her mother differently upon her mother's marriage to a Filipino. Her mother was not given even a square foot of land as inheritance despite the fact that her mother's family-owned lands in the Oroku District in Naha City. The same thing happened to her mother's youngest sister and Sylvia could not fathom the reason for this.

An Invisible Minority in Okinawan Society

Despite having Japanese nationality, I argue that the Nisei are an "invisible minority" in Okinawa. What I refer to as being "invisible" here is not necessarily connected to "numbers", but refers more to the Nisei's social recognition in Okinawa vis-à-vis their social position and legal status as Japanese nationals. The condition of being "invisible" ought to be thought of as significant in itself, as their status as Japanese nationals render them this "invisibility", that may both be a benefit or a bane to them personally, but nevertheless challenges the whole notion of being "Japanese" and "foreign" at the same time.

The "social invisibility" of the Nisei and thus their existence as an "invisible minority" in Okinawa can be thought of as caused by the following: the Japanese nationality of the Nisei and their physical features that are indistinguishable from the rest of the Okinawan population, as well as their "disembeddedness" in Okinawan society.

As expected of those who obtained Japanese nationality, the Nisei had to adopt Japanese names. Most of them used the surnames of their Okinawan mothers, and while several of them chose to retain their first names, others have adopted Japanese first names that they use in legal documentations and similar instances, while using their first names (or nicknames)—mostly Western or Christian names—in other aspects of their lives, such as in relating with friends, fellow churchgoers, and others.[2] Thus, these Nisei, being legally Japanese themselves, live their lives like many other Japanese; and due to legal status, their "difference" and their being "half" or "hāfu" tend to be inconspicuous. Their inconspicuous existence is also attributable to their physical features which, as I earlier mentioned, are indistinguishable from majority of Okinawans and hence, as opposed to the more noticeable Amerasians, they are able to "pass" as locals and thus "fit in" Okinawan society.

Then again, this "social invisibility" of the Nisei goes beyond physical attributes and legal status, but can also be explained by how they live their everyday lives and how they are "embedded" or "disembedded" in Okinawan society as a whole. A large majority of the Nisei in Okinawa work on U.S. military bases in the prefecture, while others are engaged in work related to education, such as primary and secondary school teachers. Others, meanwhile, work in service industries, such as hotels and restaurants (both on- and off-base). Thus, we can surmise that most of the daily interactions of these Nisei base workers are limited to people on base themselves, with a large number of them American military and civilian personnel, as well as Japanese employees and other nationals. Whatever is going on inside these military installations is not visible to local Okinawan eyes, and entry to these bases is only accessible to a limited number who are privileged to be related—by affinity or consanguinity—to people working on base as USFJ employees, or those who work with affiliated Japanese construction companies, or military troops themselves.

While it can be considered that their work on base contributes to their being "disembedded" in Okinawan society, the Nisei spend most of their lives outside the base interacting with their fellow Nisei and with Filipinos, most of the time in church (both Catholic and Protestant). Thus, their only interactions with local Okinawans have been mostly through their children's schools (if they enrolled them in local schools), such as during parent-teacher meetings and similar activities (Zulueta 2012: 383). There are of course Nisei who chose to have their children attend American or International Schools, many of which also cater to children of American military and service personnel.

Despite, I argue, being integrated in Okinawan society as Japanese nationals, and enjoying (legal) membership in the Japanese nation-state as well as all the social and political rights normally given to those with Japanese nationality, the Nisei's inadequate cultural and linguistic literacy contradict their legal and nominal existence as "Japanese" and hence they are considered "foreign" in Okinawan society. This reality then is significant in understanding the Nisei's "disembeddedness" in current Okinawan society.

A "Minority Within a Minority"

Notwithstanding their status as legally "Japanese", the Nisei have also pointed out their position as a "minority" in Okinawan society. Raphael once told me: "We are a minority within a minority. Okinawans are a minority in Japan, and we become a minority again within the Okinawan society." The Nisei's condition of being a "double minority" within Okinawan society negates their legal status and existence as "Japanese", since their being Japanese is not directly linked to perceptions of homogeneity and ethnicity, but rather to nationality and citizenship.

"They look at Filipinos as second-class citizens," Raphael added. Likewise, Marco Yara feels that the Nisei are also discriminated against in Okinawa. However, he thinks that Americans favour Filipinos and Nisei because they are proficient in English. He added that there are a lot of return migrants from China (*zanryūkoji*) as well as the third (*sansei*) and fourth (*yonsei*) generation *Nikkeijin* from Peru, Brazil, and other Latin American countries and they seem to be favoured as migrant workers. Marco feels that *Nikkeijin* from the Philippines, as well as the Nisei are still not being given a warm welcome.

Having Japanese nationality but not being "culturally Japanese or Okinawan" seems contradictory in a society where the myth of homogeneity still exists. Language proficiency and communication are also issues. Raphael said, "you're a Japanese that doesn't speak Japanese...you're completely lost." According to Nobuko Adachi, "language is the threshold in the creation of a social boundary between Japanese locals and Nikkei workers" (Adachi 2006: 14). Indeed, it is the insufficient knowledge of the Japanese language that creates a boundary between the local Okinawans and the Nisei in Okinawan society, relegating them to a status considered foreign despite having Okinawan parentage and Japanese nationality. Legally they are Japanese, but culturally they are not.

This also reflects the case of the Brazilian *Nikkeijin* (and other *Nikkeijin* from Latin America), wherein the "ethnic homeland", which many of them had only heard of through stories from their parents and/or grandparents, is not the homeland that they imagine it to be as they are oftentimes seen as foreign despite their Japanese ancestry upon settling in Japanese soil. Thus, many of these *Nikkeijin* are seen to occupy a "liminal" space, as they are seen as Japanese in their natal country of Brazil; while on the other hand in Japan, despite their phenotypical features, they are not considered to be Japanese due mainly to the different cultural atmosphere they grew up in, and thus they are regarded as Brazilians (Tsuda 2003).

It should also be noted here that Okinawa's place in the Japanese national polity sends forth ambivalent signals concerning Okinawan identity. As I explained in detail in Chap. 2, the subjugation of the Ryukyuan archipelago and the subsequent creation of Okinawa prefecture entailed a process of "modernization", where Okinawans were made to be "Okinawans" in the process of becoming "Japanese" (Tomiyama 1990: 3–5).

Furthermore, as I argued in Chap. 4, Okinawan identity should be understood within the context and effects of Japanese colonialism and the U.S. Occupation of the prefecture, as well as the continuing U.S. military base presence there. Okinawans are in a liminal position where they are seen as both Japanese and not Japanese. This is also the case for those who are "hāfu" or "half"—where being "hāfu" leaves them in a situation of being a "double minority" since their "hāfu" identity challenges not only what being "Japanese" is, but also what being "Okinawan" is.

For the Nisei, the claim to be Japanese and Okinawan stems from their nationality as Japanese and their Okinawan parentage. However, the seemingly narrow view of what constitutes Japanese identity and the conflation of nationality, citizenship, race, and ethnicity within the whole concept of "Japaneseness", only reinforces the "us-them" dichotomy that creates an "invisible minority" within the category of "Japanese". Due to the fact that the Nisei are not really "culturally" Japanese, they have been considered to be more "foreign"—an "Other"—in Okinawan society. This "Othering" obviously has repercussions as to how these Nisei think of where and what their home is.

HOME AND HOMES; HOME AND ROOTS

Considering the return migration of the Nisei to Okinawa as transitory and not fixed may have an impact on how they perceive what home is for them. Home, I argue, is a situational construct that it is defined according to how they construct their identities in relation to current global conditions as well as to their experience of the everyday (be it in the past or in the present). Home is also tied to notions of identity and belonging, as well as to *roots* and *routes* (Clifford 1994, 1997), with the former indicating an origin, a foundation, and one's ancestry, and the latter implying diffusion, movement, and migration (I include return migration here). Home, then, should not be regarded as a "singular homeland" (Abdelhady 2008: 66), as the case of the Nisei, having both Okinawan and Filipino parentage, contradicts this common assumption of a homeland as a singular place, such that ethnic return migration assumes the ethnic homogeneity of the returnees. As Sara Ahmed (1999) points out:

> Home is here, not a particular place that one simply inhabits, but more than one place: there are too many homes to allow place to secure the roots or routes of one's destination...The journey between homes provides the subject with the contours of a space of belonging. (Ahmed 1999: 330)

Hence, for the Nisei, to talk of home may not only refer to a home but to homes, such as they talk of returns rather than a return, as they continue to involve themselves in transnational activities.

"I have three homes", Sylvia said as she told me that she refers to Okinawa as her home. The same goes with the Philippines and with the United States that she now considers her home: "Because I am half, my home is Okinawa or the Philippines, and then when I come here (Okinawa), [and I am asked] 'oh you're going home?' 'Oh yeah, I'm going home', I mean, America. I have three homes, actually." She added that she used to come home to Okinawa every year to visit her parents when they were still alive. Sylvia's husband who used to work for United Airlines promised her that she could go home to Okinawa every year, as he knew that she initially did not want to leave her parents in Okinawa. In fact, before her mother passed away, Sylvia used to visit her every six months. With this, it can be said that what she defines as home or homes are places where personal relations are present. Home at a certain point in her life was Okinawa, since her parents were living there, but it still continues to be her home since two of her brothers live in Okinawa, and the presence of her fellow Nisei in the prefecture makes her feel "at home". In this regard, home becomes tied to one's identity and one's perception of "roots": "After like seeing my Nisei friends, we are like family because we have identity," she said. Moreover, Sylvia spoke of how she regards Oroku Catholic Church as a community since most of the parishioners are Nisei like her and that they could relate with each other since they share the same histories and sentiments. The Philippines is also home to her because of her Filipino roots and because of the presence of friends and kin. Presently, the United States has become home to her as she currently lives there with her husband and children. Home is not only defined by one's birthplace, but is also tied to one's perception/s of his or her identity, and also to feelings of belongingness.

Likewise, Vincent Shimabukuro talked about having more than one home when he mentioned that he has two. When we started talking about several issues being faced by Okinawa and Okinawans (as well as the Nisei in Okinawa), he started by saying, "back here (Okinawa)", then continued on to say, "back in the Philippines", as he talked about his wish that both Japan and the Philippines address issues that are of equal significance to them such as the plight of the children born to Japanese fathers and former Filipina entertainers. He then added, *"kung Filipino ka* (if you're Filipino), you're supposed to say, 'back in the Philippines', but in our case, this (Okinawa) is our homeland, the Philippines is homeland." For the Nisei then, home is not merely a place of return (i.e. a place of origin) or a particular destination. Nor is it solely a place of belonging. For the Nisei, as illustrated in the above cases, home is tied to notions of (ethnic) identity. Sylvia indicated that because she is "half", her home is Okinawa or the Philippines, in a similar vein, Vincent said that for them, both Okinawa and the Philippines is homeland. For these individuals who trace their roots to two places, to talk of home as a singularity is not, to say in the least, applicable, as for these Nisei, home is tied to how they see themselves and how they construct their identities in relation to particular situations.

In this regard, I would like to point out that people's perceptions of home are also linked to the concept of "situational ethnicity" (Okamura 1981). Okamura notes that individuals may "advance their claims to membership in any one of a generally limited number of ethnic categories that they belong to, or perhaps do not belong to, in accordance with their belief that such a selection of ethnic identity will be to their advantage" (Okamura 1981: 454–455). An illustration of this is the Nisei's return to Okinawa for the attainment of cultural (e.g. Japanese nationality), economic (e.g. work opportunities), and social capital, where being a person of Okinawan descent becomes advantageous to them. In Okinawa, many of them are Japanese nationals, and thus they enjoy legal rights as any other Japanese. Their much more comfortable living situations (as opposed to other migrants) and for some, their ability to communicate with the locals, imbibe in them a sense of "home" in Okinawa.

Home as tied to one's sense of self or to how one constructs his/her identity according to societal and structural factors may also be linked to the idea that identity can be regarded as a site for claims and as a site for resistance. The Nisei is in a position to claim an Okinawan identity, and in turn claim to have Okinawa as his/her home by virtue of his/her ethnicity.

For the Nisei, what they consider home, apart from feelings of belongingness, and such, is attributable to their ethnic identity—to quote Vincent once again: "in our (Nisei) case, this (Okinawa) is our homeland, the Philippines is homeland." On the other hand, identity can also be a site for resistance, in that their identity as Nisei—a product of American Occupation and labour migrations between Okinawa and the Philippines (and hence is a socio-historical construct)—has also served as a self-denomination that identifies them as different from Japanese-Filipinos, that is those who trace their roots to the Japanese mainland.

Despite saying, "deep inside me, I know I'm a Filipino", Raphael talked about how he thought of "home" as Okinawa. Upon returning to Okinawa in 1971 for a supposedly short visit since classes were called off during that time (the turbulent years of the Marcos regime), he said that he was all set to come home to Okinawa, with all the required documents at hand, only to find out that he needed a visa to go to Okinawa, which was still under U.S. Occupation. In Chap. 1, I quoted Raphael as telling me that he needed to apply for a visa "just to return to my old home". This "old home" that he was returning to indicates a concrete entity—a place where he once lived and grew up. Looking at this case, one can say that one's perception of home may be linked closely to an experience, such that home becomes an experienced event.

"Home as experience" is inextricably tied to one's experiences of the everyday. It is the "site of everyday lived experience" (Brah 1996: 4). It is also tied to one's experience of home, but is not only tied to memories of one's childhood, but also with where one is, and what or who one is (i.e. one's (self)-identification). It is the "lived experience of a locality…as mediated by the historically specific everyday of social relations" (Brah 1996: 192).

"There's no place like home", Lillian told me as she expressed her plan to (probably) return to the Philippines and retire there. Despite living in Okinawa for nearly three decades, Lillian said that since she grew up in the Philippines, "*ang puso mo ay nandoon pa rin, although feel at home na ako dito* (your heart is still there, although I already feel at home here)". It should be remembered that Lillian experienced a culture shock when she first returned to Okinawa to visit her relatives in Naha. She said that Naha was too Japanese for her and that her relatives are very much different from her because of cultural differences. However, Lillian already "feels at home" in Okinawa (Ginowan City in particular) since the "multi-cultural make-up" of the place where she lives and her daily contact with Okinawans,

Japanese, Filipinos, Americans, and fellow Nisei, gives her a sense of home, even though her "heart" is in the Philippines. Indeed, "home is where the heart is", but is the heart always at home?

Home then for the Nisei is both Okinawa and the Philippines. Having *roots* in both Okinawa and the Philippines, the Nisei are in a position to "shuttle" between these two locations when they ply their *routes* as they construct their home. However, what home is to one person may not mean the same to another; and for the Nisei, notions of home are tied not only to perceptions about their ethnic identity, but also to mobility, which is largely dependent on capital (cultural and social) and social—as well as legal—status.

Moreover, the conception and perception of home for these Nisei relates more often than not, to their hybridity, which oftentimes, if not always, posits ambivalences in one's identity. These so-called hybrid identities, exhibiting not only dual but also multiple identifications, are always in flux, not to mention the ambivalences that generally characterize such identities. Zygmunt Bauman said that: "In a liquid modern setting of life, identities are perhaps the most common, most acute, most deeply felt and troublesome incarnations of ambivalence" (Bauman 2004: 32). For some individuals, identities are created in a place that one considers home. In some instances, others create or have constructed their identities in another place that has become conflated with home. In this sense, home is seen to be linked to *roots* but this link was achieved through *routes*, that is the migrant's (or return migrant's) journey/s in the process of his/her self-actualization, as he/she appropriates his/her transmigratory character largely made possible through his/her cultural and social capital. It can be said then that identity is "less about *rootedness*, but more about *routedness* (emphasis included in text)" (Espiritu 2008: 97).

"Home" and "Homing"

How then are homes made in the process of migration, or in this case, in the process of return? How are homes made and/or experienced upon one's return?

For people of Okinawan descent and the *Nikkeijin*, the return to Japan is mainly driven by the economic situation in their countries (i.e. Brazil, Peru, the Philippines, etc.) and is in part aided by the revision of the Immigration Control and Refugee Recognition Act in 1990, which saw a rapid increase in the population of Japanese-Brazilians in Japan. For the

Nisei, aside from the economic and political conditions in the Philippines, the continued U.S. base presence in the prefecture, which entails the demand for base labour, has also been instrumental in the return migration of the Nisei, who invest on their cultural and social capital to land in coveted base jobs. This condition also brought about new conceptions of "home" for the Nisei—whether home is Okinawa or the Philippines. Home, which is not a fixed entity in itself—due to the "transitory" character of return—can be said to be flexible and/or impermanent as it is dependent on the migrant's place in society, that is, one's legal and social status, as well as on his/her sense of belongingness. John Urry states that almost all dwellings "involve complex relationships between belongingness and travelling, within and beyond the boundaries of national societies" (Urry 2000: 157) and that these "dwellings are often impermanent" (Ibid: 144).

Here, I look at the concept of "homing", which refers to "people's *evolving potential to attach a sense of home to their life circumstances, in light of their assets and of the external structure of opportunities* (emphasis in original)" (Boccagni 2017: 23). For these Nisei, "homing" entails following the customs and traditions in Okinawa, if one desires to be "at home" there. Meryl Miyazato, for instance, believes that since she is in Okinawa, she has to be involved in Okinawan things and customs. She also thinks that Filipinos and Nisei have to follow the customs in Okinawa or try to follow them, and laments the fact that others do not. "I live here, I have to (follow customs)," she told me. Moreover, she does not understand why some Filipinos and Nisei do not follow nor do they even try to follow those customs, as she believes that reflects back to how Filipinos and Nisei are and how they would be perceived. "There are some things that you have to follow; there are some things of course, [where] you have to assert your individuality. It still depends on the situation, I guess." For his part, Sonny Uechi said that to adjust to life in Okinawa one must "do what the Romans do"—"When you are in Japan, you act like a Japanese. When you are in the Philippines, you act like a Filipino." Himself acting upon his advice, he said that he "survived" the years he spent in Okinawa, and is prepared for the years that would still come his way.

I also argue that "homing" or the process of "home-building" or "home-making" is not merely a self-fashioning act tied to one's sense of a home (which may entail a search for one's home), but is also linked to processes of constructing and/or re-constructing social relations that link one's idea of home in the past to one's notion of home in the future. In other words, "homing" is not a personal act of "home-making" exclusively for the self, but is also related to "home-building" in relation to others—be it one's immediate family, one's community, or a larger society. "Homing", as influenced by societal and structural factors, is inherently a social act. It is "attaching a sense of home" in "light of one's structure of opportunities" (Boccagni 2017: 23).

In the process of their own "home-making", some Nisei have involved themselves in several cause-oriented activities, one of which is assisting Filipino migrant workers in Okinawa. This act on the part of the Nisei is transposed onto a community of migrant Filipinos (non-Nisei), as the Nisei identifies with them due to a shared ancestry owing to their part-Filipino parentage. This, coupled with the Nisei's legal status and cultural and social capital, enable them to be involved in these kinds of activities.

For his part, Raphael has been involved in activities that assist Filipino migrant workers in Okinawa. Due to a language handicap, it cannot be denied that Filipinos, as well as the Nisei, encounter some problems with regards to Japanese laws and regulations as well as government policies. One of these is Japan's retirement policy. Raphael is involved in disseminating information about Japan's retirement policy, particularly in the translation of pertinent documents about this. He has also been involved in requesting the prefectural government for assistance in the Japanese language education of Filipinos and the Nisei. He said, "we fight for Filipino's rights over here; we can do that because we're citizens also, we can speak out... and we don't have to worry about the visa problem." With this, it is apparent that he uses his Japanese nationality as symbolic capital (Bourdieu 1926) in order for him to help out Filipinos in Okinawa.

Moreover, the "home-making" that the Nisei engage in is also sometimes transposed onto a minority population, in this case, Filipino migrant workers. Despite the legal and economic status that the Nisei enjoy, they see themselves as instrumental in upholding migrant Filipinos' rights, as they themselves trace part of their roots to the Philippines. In this regard, one can say that the Nisei engage in creating a home for themselves by making, or working to make Okinawa a comfortable place not only for themselves, but also for these migrants.

For the Nisei, their return (which is more often than not, transitory) and their "home-making" are part and parcel of their lives as they traverse both the Philippines and Okinawa in accordance with current social, economic, political, and global conditions. Their return and their perceptions of home are in conjunction with how they negotiate their notion of "routes" and "roots". In some cases, home may actually be nowhere as it is in two or more locations, or everywhere. I end this chapter with literary scholar, bell hooks' (1990) quote:

> At times, home is nowhere. At times, one knows only the extreme estrangement and alienation. Then home is no longer just one place. It is locations. Home is that place which enables and promotes varied and ever changing perspectives, a place where one discovers new ways of seeing reality, frontiers of difference. (hooks 1990: 148)

Notes

1. In my interviews with Nisei residing in Metro Manila in 2003, and in Okinawa in 2007 and 2010, both groups reported incidences of discrimination from the locals. However, I also found out that discriminatory behaviour among the locals, particularly in the Philippines, varied according to the Nisei's geographic location (i.e. region) and the period/year of birth (i.e. Filipinos' discrimination towards the Japanese was more intense in the immediate post-war years than in the late 1960s).
2. The requirement to adopt a Japanese name has been removed with the 1985 amendment to the Nationality Act. However, it was said that the Ministry of Justice "recommended" that applicants adopt Japanese names. This unofficial policy has been enforced at the local level (See Chung 2010: 20).

References

Abdelhady, D. (2008). Representing the Homeland: Lebanese Diasporic Notions of Home and Return in a Global Context. *Cultural Dynamics, 20*(1), 53–72.

Adachi, N. (2006). Introduction: Theorizing Japanese Diaspora. In N. Adachi (Ed.), *Japanese Diasporas: Unsung Pasts, Conflicting Presents, and Uncertain Futures* (pp. 1–22). London: Routledge.

Ahmed, S. (1999). Home and Away: Narratives of Migration and Estrangement. *International Journal of Cultural Studies, 2*(3), 329–347.

Bourdieu, P. (1926). The forms of capital. In J. Richardson (Ed.), *Handbook of Theory of Research for the Sociology of Education* (pp. 46–58). New York: Greenwood Press.

Bauman, Z. (2004). *Identity: Conversations with Benedetto Vecchi*. Cambridge: Polity Press.

Boccagni, P. (2017). *Migration and the Search for Home: Mapping Domestic Space in Migrants' Everyday Lives*. New York: Palgrave Macmillan.

Brah, A. (1996). *Cartographies of Diaspora: Contesting Identities.* London: Routledge.
Chambers, I. (1994). *Migrancy, Culture, Identity.* London: Routledge.
Chung, E. A. (2010). *Immigration and Citizenship in Japan.* New York: Cambridge University Press.
Clifford, J. (1994). Diasporas. *Cultural Anthropology, 9*(3), 302–338.
Clifford, J. (1997). *Routes: Travel and Translation in the Late Twentieth Century.* Cambridge: Harvard University Press.
Espiritu, Y. L. (2008). *Homebound: Filipino American Lives Across Cultures, Communities, and Countries* (Philippine ed.). Quezon City: Ateneo de Manila University Press.
hooks, b. (1990). *Yearning: Race, Gender, and Cultural Politics.* Boston: South End Press.
Iyotani, T. (Ed.). (2007). *Idō kara Basho wo Tō: Gendai Imin Kenkyū no Kadai (Motion in Place/Place in Motion).* Tokyo: Yushindo Kōbunsha.
Massey, D. (1994). *Space, Place, and Gender.* Cambridge: Polity Press.
Moreton-Robinson, A. (2003). I Still Call Australia Home: Indigenous Belonging and Place in a White Postcolonizing Society. In S. Ahmed, C. Castaneda, A. Fortier, & M. Sheller (Eds.), *Uprootings/Regroundings: Questions of Home and Migration* (pp. 23–40). Oxford: Berg.
Newbold, K. B. (2001). Counting Migrants and Migrations: Comparing Lifetime and Fixed-Interval Return and Onward Migration. *Economic Geography, 77*(1), 23–40.
Okamura, J. (1981). Situational ethnicity. *Ethnic and Racial Studies, 4*(4), 452–465.
Parreñas, R. S. (2003). *Servants of Globalization: Women, Migration, and Domestic Work* (Philippine ed.). Quezon City: Ateneo de Manila University Press.
Tomiyama, I. (1990). *Kindai Nihon Shakai to "Okinawajin": Nihonjin ni naru to iu koto.* Tokyo: Nihon Keizai Hyōronsha.
Tsuda, T. (2003). *Strangers in the Ethnic Homeland: Japanese Brazilian Return Migration in Transnational Perspective.* New York: Columbia University Press.
Urry, J. (2000). *Sociology Beyond Societies: Mobilities for the Twenty-First Century.* London: Routledge.
Zulueta, J. O. (2012). Living as Migrants in a Place That Was Once "Home": The Nisei, the U.S. Bases, and Okinawan Society. *Philippine Studies: Historical and Ethnographic Viewpoints, 60*(3), 367–390.

CHAPTER 8

Future Trajectories: A Conclusion

Nisei Futures

One rainy day in September 2018, I had dinner with Stephanie Ojana at a restaurant at the American Village in Chatan Town. This American Village is popular among tourists—domestic tourists especially—as it gives one a "taste" of being in the United States, with its "American" restaurants and shops in this small shopping/leisure space. Chatan Town is also host to a part of Kadena Airbase, and on weekends one would notice U.S. servicemen walking around the American Village. It was a decade since I last saw her and when we finally met up at the Starbucks near the entrance before heading to the restaurant, she gave me a hug. She still remembers me after all these years.

Stephanie has since retired from her job as a manager at a fast-food outlet on base in 2013. She was actually offered a five-year extension for her AAFES (Army and Air Force Exchange Services) job, but did not accept it as she told me work was stressful. Retirement age for USFJ work is 60 years. Now, she works part-time at a school cafeteria on weekdays from 7:30 in the morning to around 1:00 in the afternoon, at the same time taking care of her 86-year-old mother. Showing me photos of her mother and her daughter, she told me that she takes care of her mother when she comes back from her cafeteria work, and that her daughter is now working at a telecommunications company in the prefecture. She also shared that she has not been to the Philippines for 23 years, and only

---

© The Author(s) 2020
J. O. Zulueta, *Transnational Identities on Okinawa's Military Bases*,
https://doi.org/10.1007/978-981-32-9787-6_8

recently went there to attend a wedding. Stephanie also shared that she does not see herself going home to the Philippines for good.

Bobby Katsukata had the same sentiment when I spoke to him back in December 2012 at his home in Chatan Town. He was two years short of retiring from his work on base and told me then that he does not plan to return to the Philippines after he retires. Rather, he would like to take the opportunity upon retirement to travel and see more of the world. According to him, "Okinawa is for me," thus indicating that he will most likely stay in the prefecture for good. Sonny Uechi, who at first was a little hesitant to go to Okinawa as he was living a comfortable life in his native Cebu in the central Philippines, made the return to his birthplace due to the prodding of his friends, who told him that life in Okinawa is economically more secure. When I spoke to him in March 2010, he told me that he does not see himself returning to the Philippines after retirement as he has more rights and benefits as a Japanese national. He also has his family with him in Okinawa.

Meanwhile, I also met up with Meryl Miyazato in September 2018 in Naha City, and she shared that she has a year left before she retires from her HR (human resources)-related work at the Marine Corps Community Services or MCCS. She plans to extend her stay though until she reaches 65 years (which is the maximum age allowed for extension), as she thinks she might get bored upon retirement. Like Stephanie, Bobby, and Sonny, she does not see herself going back to the Philippines for good. Okinawa is home to her since her family—her children and grandchildren—are in Okinawa (this is despite the fact that her Okinawan mother is in the Philippines living with her other siblings).[1]

Raphael Miyagi spends his retirement years helping the Filipino community in Okinawa. He also has his own travel business where he brings Okinawan tourists to the Philippines regularly. Whenever I meet him on my visits to Okinawa, I ask him whether he still intends to go back to the Philippines. He said no. He sees spending his retirement years in the prefecture as his children and grandchildren are in Okinawa. This was what he told me again when I saw him in September 2018.

What then lies ahead for these Nisei currently living in Okinawa? The cases above show that most, if not all, of these Nisei returnees in Okinawa see themselves remaining in the prefecture until after their retirement, and most likely, throughout their lives. These sentiments were also echoed by the other Nisei who I have spoken to and met throughout the course of my study—at churches, at parties, and other gatherings. This is expected as these Nisei enjoy the privileges of being a Japanese national, and thus are not seen as "foreign", in a legal sense. As I discussed in earlier chapters, these Nisei also enjoy an amount of social mobility due to their employment on base as well as their legal rights as Japanese nationals. Thus, from a materialist perspective, one can expect that these Nisei will remain in Okinawa after retirement. As these Nisei enjoy a more privileged status—both legally and economically—their future is more certain than other returnees (such as the Japanese-Brazilians working in factories and engaged in low-skilled work in the Japanese mainland) and foreign migrants in the prefecture.

Do they see the same futures for their *sansei* (third generation) children and their *yonsei* (fourth generation) grandchildren? When I spoke to these Nisei about their *sansei* children, and whether they would want them to follow in their footsteps and be USFJ employees themselves, most of them did not wish base employment on their children. Rather, they prefer that their children work elsewhere. Nevertheless, there are some *sansei* who work on base as USFJ employees like their Nisei parents. While I have not looked into the *sansei* population engaged in base work, this phenomenon would open up significant avenues for further investigation, where base work seemingly is "reproduced" inter-generationally within this particular ethnic group.

The future of base employment also depends on the continued existence of U.S. military bases in Okinawa and the whole Japanese archipelago. However, it is too soon to say if the bases will indeed disappear in several years' time. While there are people who desire the ouster of the bases, there are also those who consider the base presence as part of their lives, not to mention, as a source of their livelihood. This group obviously includes the USFJ employees. During my trips and short stays in Okinawa, I also spoke to other people—locals, non-Nisei, taxi drivers, activists, shop and restaurant employees, students—and asked them about their thoughts and opinions on the U.S. base presence. Their perceptions on the existence of these military installations in their midst are very much varied and show a schism in this whole issue. It is probably safe to say that the status quo will be maintained a bit longer and that the stipulations in the U.S.-Japan Security Treaty will remain.

Okinawan Society and the U.S. Bases

Upon Japan's defeat in the Second World War, the United States occupied Japan from 1945–1952, with the southernmost prefecture of Okinawa occupied for 20 more years, until 1972. A significant development during this period was the construction of U.S. military bases in Japan, where majority of these installations is concentrated in the southernmost prefecture of Okinawa (at present, around 70 per cent of these bases still exists on the main island of Okinawa). Due to Okinawa's strategic location in the region, as well as to contain the communist threat during the Cold War, not to mention the increase in base construction that coincided during the Korean War (Iacobelli 2018), Okinawa still hosts the largest number of U.S. military bases in the East Asian region.

The existence of U.S. military bases on the Japanese mainland and Okinawa, while largely believed to provide security in the region and regarded as a source of employment for the local populace, also invites other contentious issues such as environmental problems, noise pollution, crimes, traffic accidents, and others. It is a double-edged sword.

Indeed, the U.S. presence on Okinawan soil during the immediate post-war years brought about socio-cultural changes in Okinawan society that have had repercussions not only on the prefecture's socio-cultural environment, but also at how Okinawans see themselves vis-à-vis the occupying forces and the Japanese mainland. These military bases can be thought of as "contact zones" (Pratt 1992) that enable interactions between the locals and the U.S. military, and in this context, between the victors and the defeated. Here, I borrow May Louise Pratt's concept where she defines contact zones as "social spaces where disparate cultures meet, clash, and grapple with each other, often in highly asymmetrical relations of domination and subordination—such as colonialism and slavery, or their aftermaths as they are lived out across the globe today" (Pratt 1992: 7).

The presence of military bases promotes "close socio-economic interactions" with the host society and these social interactions such as love affairs, marriage, and cultural exchanges are developed between military personnel and the locals (Yamazaki 2011: 254). With the U.S. bases in Okinawa, socio-cultural and economic interactions are to be expected; these interactions have also occurred through cultural and interpersonal interactions, trade (not to mention the black market that thrived in Okinawa during the Occupation period), romantic relationships—mostly between local women and the men of the Occupying Forces—and births from these unions, not to mention conflict between military personnel and the locals that were intertwined with issues associated with racial/ethnic discrimination and unequal power relationships (manifested mostly in cases of power harassment and sexual abuse).

These "close socio-economic interactions" also occurred as an outcome of this whole transnational project of military basing. As I argued in previous chapters, the Occupation of Okinawa should be seen as a transnational project that brought in other players—albeit peripheral—to the whole U.S.-Japan/Okinawa relations during the immediate post-war years. This is illustrated by the presence of an international workforce for the construction and operations of these military bases. Third Country Nationals or TCNs where brought in from other countries such as the Philippines, China, and India, to assist and provide additional labour that could not be addressed by LNs or local nationals. Most of these recruits were male and, like U.S. servicemen during this time, they met and had romantic affairs with local Okinawan women. This was the period that significantly saw the creation of the Amerasian or the offspring of American servicemen and Asian women (in this case, Okinawan women), as well as other offspring of intermarriages between local women and the Occupying Forces, including the TCNs. This book focused on the offspring of Filipino TCNs and Okinawan women, who identify themselves as Nisei or second generation, pointing to their Okinawan parentage. Born in Okinawa and moving during their childhood years to their father's home country upon the termination of their fathers' work contracts, a significant population of these Nisei began returning to their birthplace as early as the 1970s, as adults. Most of these Nisei sought work on base—a lucrative employment opportunity that gave them social mobility, sparing them as well from being relegated to low-skilled work had they been employed off-base. With their ethnicity that functioned as cultural capital, which in turn translated into the acquisition of Japanese nationality, in addition to their proficiency in English, these Nisei were able to find employment on base, reminiscent of their fathers who worked on these same bases as TCNs in the immediate post-war years. In what seems to be a reproduction of base labour, these Nisei work instead as United States Forces in Japan employees (USFJ employees) employed by the Government of Japan, under the banner of the U.S.-Japan Security Treaty.

As I pointed out in Chap. 4, these Nisei returnees challenge the concept of who and what a Japanese/Okinawan is. Their nationality as Japanese defines them as such, but their part-Filipino parentage points to their cultural difference, thus they are seen as not "completely" Japanese/Okinawan. This is compounded by their lack of Japanese language proficiency particularly in reading and writing. Thus, they are seen as a "minority" within Okinawan society—a minority status that they seem to share with other "hāfus" such as the Amerasian; however, in the case of the Nisei, their "difference" is less conspicuous. Moreover, the Nisei's case also presents stimulating discussions on return migration and the notion of home, topics that I explored and discussed in Chaps. 5 and 7, where I argue that the return of the Nisei can be seen as transitory, and that their perceptions of what and where home is, is tied how they construct their identity in relation to social, structural, and global conditions. Home is a situational construct and return is the process by which these individuals negotiate their idea of "routes" and "roots" (Clifford 1994, 1997). While most of these Nisei envision themselves staying in Okinawa well into their future, for most of them, home is both Okinawa and the Philippines—two places where they trace their roots. Thus, it can be said that "roots" and "routes" for these Nisei continually shape and re-shape, define and re-define, where and what their home is, which in the end is closely tied to one's identity and sense of belonging.

Looking Beyond the Barbed Wire Fence

As I earlier mentioned, the U.S. bases in Okinawa and Japan can be thought of as "contact zones"—cultural and social zones of contact between occupier and the occupied (Fehrenbach 2005: 17). The American Occupation of Japan and Okinawa, as well as other areas of the world during the aftermath of the Second World War saw these "asymmetrical relations" (Pratt 1992: 7) between the victor and the defeated, and the occupiers and the local population of the areas they occupied. However, to consider the U.S. army solely as the "occupiers" will leave out other actors who have been involved in the Occupation project, such as the TCNs.

Bases in Okinawa and the Japanese mainland can be said to have become a part of the daily lives of individuals and the community. In my previous trips to Okinawa, I was able to talk to some individuals—both young and old—who consider the base presence as part of their everyday lives; something that has become "normal", especially for the much younger generations who were born after the War. Cynthia Enloe suggests that these bases have "draped themselves with the camouflage of normalcy" (Enloe 2000: 66), where the community and its individuals have accepted the presence of these bases and see these military installations as "valuable", since these translate into jobs as well as business opportunities within and without the bases.

Whatever image the locals have of these U.S. bases, these military installations are usually seen as "static" places (or spaces). People regard these bases as enclaves as well since while they exist and occupy land in the host country (at some point through usurpation, such as in the Diego Garcia case), they are very much separate and apart from the local community. However, locals have to contend with the presence of these bases and many of these base towns have taken on a character of their own. Many of the locals also work on bases stationed in their towns or cities. Hence, these military bases can (and should) also be seen in the context of mobilities (Sheller and Urry 2006), where one witnesses not only flows of information, army/military personnel and their families, base workers, goods, and services, but also of cultural flows (the development of jazz music in post-war Okinawa is closely associated with the American Occupation, and many of the musicians in the 1950s and 1960s who played in clubs catering to American soldiers were Filipinos (Roberson 2011: 598)). Furthermore, military troops are also able to move between and among bases. This was what I attempted to illustrate in this book, where I looked at the flows of labour and various types of migrants in and out of Okinawa from the Occupation Period to contemporary times.

As is largely known, the U.S. presence in Okinawa has also sparked issues regarding sovereignty and human rights, as well as environmental issues that are largely connected to the presence of a large number of military installations in the prefecture. This issue also calls for transnational activism and solidarity. Thus, it is imperative for current and future scholars to be more aware of the significance of other actors, both state and non-state, in our understanding of Japan and Okinawa in the context of U.S. military basing—actors that may have been and continue to exist in the periphery, yet hold much significance in our understanding of this reality.

Note

1. Apart from the fact that some of her children are in the Philippines, Meryl's mother does not want to return to Okinawa since she does not have a tomb there as her husband is Filipino. Traditionally, Okinawan women are supposed to be buried in their husband's tomb when they die. This is one issue faced by the Okinawan wives of the Filipino TCNs upon their return to Okinawa, thus, not a few of them decide to remain in the Philippines. I explored this issue in an earlier article (See Zulueta 2016).

References

Clifford, J. (1994). Diasporas. *Cultural Anthropology, 9*(3), 302–338.
Clifford, J. (1997). *Routes: Travel and Translation in the Late Twentieth Century.* Cambridge: Harvard University Press.
Enloe, C. (2000). *Bananas, Beaches, and Bases: Making Feminist Sense of International Politics.* Berkeley: University of California Press.
Fehrenbach, H. (2005). *Race after Hitler: Black Occupation Children in Postwar Germany and America.* Princeton: University Press.
Iacobelli, P. (2018). Okinawa and the Fear of World War Three. In T. Morris-Suzuki (Ed.), *The Korean War in Asia: A Hidden History* (pp. 109–128). Lanham: Rowman & Littlefield.
Pratt, M. L. (1992). *Imperial Eyes: Travel Writing and Transculturation.* London: Routledge.
Roberson, J. E. (2011). Doin' Our Thing: Identity and Colonial Modernity in Okinawan Rock Music. *Popular Music and Society, 34*(5), 593–620.
Sheller, M., & Urry, J. (2006). The New Mobilities Paradigm. *Environment and Planning, 38*, 207–226.
Yamazaki, T. (2011). The U.S. Militarization of a "Host" Civilian Society: The Case of Postwar Okinawa, Japan. In K. Scott & C. Flint (Eds.), *Reconstructing Conflict: Integrating War and Post-war Geographies* (pp. 253–272). Surrey: Ashgate.
Zulueta, J. O. (2016). When Death Becomes Her Question: Death, Identity, and Perceptions of Home Among Okinawan Women Return Migrants. *Mortality: Promoting the Interdisciplinary Study of Death and Dying, 21*(1), 52–70.

Index[1]

A
Aerospace Medical Squadron (AMDS/SGPM), 89
African-Americans, 46
Allied Forces, 25, 67
Amerasian, 8, 16, 32, 53, 61, 63–65, 81, 82, 106, 121, 122
American Village, 117
Army and Air Force Exchange Service (AAFES), 89, 117
Asia-Pacific, 3, 15, 16, 18, 23, 24, 28, 34, 40, 41, 48, 83
Assimilation, 26, 101

B
Base work, 7, 10, 15, 17, 18, 41–44, 50–53, 68, 91–94, 96, 97, 119
Battle of Okinawa, 25, 27
Belongingness, 5, 62, 100, 101, 109, 111, 113
Border, 75, 79, 85, 100

C
Camp Kinser, 2, 21, 91, 104
Capital
 accumulation, 17, 50, 74, 77
 ownership, 74, 77, 79
Chatan Town, 14, 32, 117, 118
Citizenship, 11, 44, 48, 58, 69, 78, 81, 107, 108
Civilian base workers, 9, 16, 41
Colonial dictatorship, 29
Colonization, 29, 41
Communism, 27–30
 communist threat, 23, 28, 120
Consanguinity, 59, 62, 69, 106
Contact zones, 41, 120, 122
Contracts, 2, 3, 7, 17, 42, 45, 48, 51, 60, 67, 88, 89, 91, 121
Cultural assimilation, 26
Cultural capital, 13, 17, 43, 49, 50, 62, 76, 77, 80, 84, 97, 121
Cultural differences, 18, 26, 65, 111, 122
Cultural identity, 10

---

[1] Note: Page numbers followed by 'n' refer to notes.

D

Dekasegi, 58
Diasporic, 74
Diego Garcia, 33, 123
Discrimination, 26, 51, 52, 63, 65, 67, 68, 96, 97, 101, 105, 115n1, 121
Double minority, 107, 108

E

East Asia, 4, 5, 8, 9, 15, 21–34, 41, 60
Economic capital, 13, 50, 77
Economic mobility, 50, 75
English
  proficiency, 46, 92
  skills, 93
Ethnic group, 8, 13, 59–62, 100, 119
Ethnic homogeneity, 109
Ethnic identity, 8, 13, 61, 62, 76, 110–112
Ethnicity, 6, 10, 13, 17, 50, 64, 69, 74, 79, 81, 101, 102, 107, 108, 110, 121
Ethnic "purity," 16
Ethnic return migration, 10, 12, 74, 75, 77, 109
Exclusion, 69

F

Filipinos, 1–4, 6–8, 10, 11, 13, 14, 39–41, 43–53, 53n2, 58–63, 65, 67–69, 78, 79, 81, 82, 92–96, 97n2, 102, 104–110, 112–114, 115n1, 118, 121, 123, 123n1
Financial difficulties, 49
Financial stability, 49, 75, 84
Flexible citizenship, 79
Futenma Air Base, 2, 21

G

Gaikokujin, 62
Gendered hierarchies, 52
Geopolitical, 6, 15, 22
Ginowan City, 2, 14, 21, 32, 53n2, 111
Global inequality of citizenship, 48
Global South, 41, 78
Gosei, 58

H

Hāfu, 16, 53, 58, 61, 62, 65, 69, 106, 108
Henoko, 21, 32
Hierarchies, 6, 40–44, 47, 50–52, 64, 66–68
High-skilled, 64
Himeyuri Monument, 27
Hōgen, 57
Hōgen fuda, 26
Home, 1, 3, 11–15, 17, 21, 42, 43, 48, 49, 58, 67, 73–75, 83, 97, 99–115, 118, 121, 122
Homeland, 10–12, 31, 73–75, 77, 100, 101, 104, 107, 108, 110, 111
Homing, 112–115
Homogeneity, 69, 107
Host country, 10, 23, 42, 49, 58, 59, 73, 79, 123
Host nation support (HNS), 90

I

Identity, 5, 10, 12–14, 16, 18n3, 30, 51, 53, 57–59, 61–63, 66–69, 73, 76, 81, 100–102, 108–112, 114, 121, 122
Ijinshu, 62
Illegitimate, 80–83
Iminzoku, 62
Immigration Control and Refugee Recognition Act (ICRRA), 76, 112

INDEX

Indirect Hire Agreement (IHA), 52, 88, 89, 91, 93
Inequalities, 6, 7, 43, 44, 50
Invisible minority, 17, 64, 99–115
Islamic fundamentalism, 23, 24
Issei, 14, 58–61

J

Japan, 1, 5, 7–10, 15–18, 21, 22, 24–34, 35n2, 40, 44, 49, 51, 52, 57, 59, 61, 62, 64, 66, 68, 69, 74–83, 85n1, 85n2, 107, 110, 112–114, 120–123
Japanese
  economy, 77
  society, 26, 27, 29
Japanese-Filipino Children/Youth (JFC/JFY), 61
Jazz, 22, 49, 123

K

Kadena Airbase, 3, 14, 22, 117
Keystone of the Pacific, 29
Kingdom of the Ryukyus, 10, 25, 57
Kita Nakagusuku Village, 14
koseki, 80–82
  koseki tōhon, 80, 82
Koza City, 2

L

Labour Management Organization/Incorporated Administrative Agency (LMO/IAA), 17, 87, 88
Labour migration, 73, 111
Language Allowance Degree (LAD), 92, 93
Local Nationals (LNs), 4, 6, 12, 41–43, 49, 51, 52, 121
Lower-middle class, 49
Low-skilled, 17, 50, 53, 64, 66, 69, 92, 119, 121

M

Marine Corps Air Station Futenma (MCAS Futenma), 21
Marine Corps Community Services (MCCS), 89, 118
Mariner's Contract (MC), 88, 89
Masculinities, 51
Master Labour Contract (MLC), 52, 88, 89, 91
Matrilineal acquisition, 80, 81
Memory, 13, 22, 60, 75, 101–104, 111
Middle-class, 49, 78, 101
Migration, 5–18, 40, 45, 50, 57, 59–62, 66, 68, 73–80, 83–85, 99, 100, 102, 103, 108, 109, 112, 113, 122
Migrant workers, 34, 58, 107, 114
Military bases, 1, 4–10, 12, 13, 16–18, 21–34, 40, 41, 44, 48, 52, 53, 63, 65, 82, 87, 89, 95, 108, 119–121, 123
  military basing, 9, 12, 16, 18, 41, 62, 64, 121
Military colony, 7, 29
Military installations, 2, 4, 6–9, 15, 17, 18, 21–24, 28, 32, 34, 40, 41, 43, 44, 48, 49, 51, 57, 59, 83, 87, 88, 91, 92, 94, 96, 106, 119, 122, 123
Ministry of Defence (Japan), 8, 15, 17, 87, 88, 93
Minority, 41, 64, 99–115, 122
Mixed identities, 58, 61–63, 66–69
Mixed race, 57–69
Mobility, 8, 15, 17, 50, 68, 73–85, 112, 119, 121, 123
Musician, 40, 44, 49, 50, 95, 123

N

Nago City, 21
Naha City, 14, 63, 69n3, 95, 105, 118
Nationality, 3, 4, 6, 9, 12, 17, 18, 43, 48, 50, 53n2, 61, 62, 64–66, 68, 69, 76, 78–84, 89, 90, 92, 94, 102, 103, 105–108, 110, 114, 121
Nation-state, 5, 65, 79, 85, 100, 106
Networks
 kinship, 5, 75, 78, 79
 social, 73, 79
Nihonjin, 62
Nikkeijin, 6, 10, 57, 58, 61, 75, 76, 82, 92, 102, 107, 112
Nisei, 5, 7, 9–14, 16, 17, 18n3, 19n5, 45, 57–69, 74–84, 89, 92–97, 97n2, 99–114, 115n1, 117–123
Non-returnee, 84, 85

O

Okinawa
 Okinawan identity, 30, 101, 108, 110
 Okinawans, 1–13, 16–18, 22, 23, 25–34, 43, 44, 46–48, 50–53, 57–63, 65–69, 76–80, 83, 84, 91, 92, 95, 97, 101, 102, 104–108, 110–113, 118, 120–122, 123n1
Okinawa City, 2, 3, 14, 22
"Other," 8, 12, 16, 49–51, 53, 57–69, 108
"Othering," 108

P

Parentage, 4, 5, 9, 10, 13, 17, 58, 59, 65, 66, 76, 78, 79, 92, 101, 107, 108, 114, 121
Passport, 8, 62, 76, 78–83
Patrilineal, 80, 81
Peripheral, 13, 25, 60, 66, 83, 121
Personal service agreement (PSA), 42
Personal service contract (PSC), 42
Philippine Okinawan Society (POS), 59, 60, 69n2, 79
Philippines, 1–3, 5–14, 16, 19n4, 19n5, 26, 28, 35n5, 39–41, 43, 45, 46, 48, 49, 57–62, 66, 67, 69, 69n1, 74, 76–84, 85n1, 93, 95, 96, 101–104, 107, 109–114, 115n1, 117, 118, 121, 122, 123n1
Philippine Scouts, 46, 59
Point of destination, 102
Point of origin, 100, 102
Post-war, 5–7, 11, 13, 14, 16, 22, 25–32, 40, 42–44, 50, 53, 53n2, 57, 60, 62, 63, 67–69, 81, 97, 101, 115n1, 120, 121, 123

R

Race
 racial, 16, 41, 43, 51, 52, 64, 66, 121
 racialization, 50–53, 62, 66, 67
 racial minorities, 41
Re-racialization, 66–69
Retirement, 18, 114, 117–119
Return migration, 8, 10, 12, 13, 17, 68, 73–80, 83, 84, 99, 108, 109, 113, 122
 returnees, 10, 11, 75, 109
Reversion of Okinawa, 51
Roots, 9, 12, 57, 60–62, 65, 76, 83, 108–112, 114, 115, 122
Routes, 3, 12, 108, 109, 112, 115, 122
Ryukyu, 10, 30
 Ryukyuan traditions, 26

INDEX

S
San Francisco Peace Treaty, 28, 29
Sansei, 58–60, 84, 107, 119
Seamen's Club, 95
Semi-skilled, 5, 6, 8, 17, 45, 59, 64, 88
Severance pay, 52
Situational construct, 12, 108, 122
Situational ethnicity, 110
Social invisibility, 105, 106
Socio-political, 6, 10, 60
South-North migration, 6
Sovereign state, 29
  sovereignty, 29
Status of Forces Agreement (SOFA), 50, 52

T
Teijūsha, 76, 82
Terrorism, 23, 24
Third Country Nationals (TCNs), 4, 6, 7, 9, 12–14, 16, 39–53, 67, 96, 121, 122, 123n1
Transnational
  movements, 5, 16, 34, 39–53
  project, 12, 16, 34, 41, 121
Typhoon of Steel, 27

U
United States Civil Administration of the Ryukyus (USCAR), 9, 18n2, 25, 44, 59

United States Forces in Japan (USFJ)
United States Forces in Japan Employees (USFJ Employees), 9, 12, 14, 16–18, 106, 119, 121
Urasoe City, 2, 21
U.S.-Japan Security Treaty, 5, 9, 15, 28, 57, 88, 119, 121
U.S. military bases, 1, 4–6, 8, 9, 12, 13, 16, 17, 22, 23, 27, 31, 33, 34, 35n1, 40, 41, 44, 53, 63, 65, 89, 106, 108, 119, 120
U.S. Occupation Forces, 1, 27, 48, 60

V
Vietnam War, 30

W
White-collar, 44, 45
World Uchinānchu Festival, 84
World War II, 24, 25, 27, 46, 49, 101, 120, 122

Y
Yokosuka Naval Base, 90
Yonsei, 58, 107, 119

Printed in the United States
By Bookmasters